Gwendolyn MacEwen

VOLUME TWO

The Later Years

Gwendolyn MacEwen

VOLUME TWO
The Later Years

Edited by Margaret Atwood
and Barry Callaghan

Introduction and Introductory Notes
by Rosemary Sullivan

Exile Editions
1994

This edition is published by Exile Editions Limited,
20 Dale Avenue, Toronto, Ontario, Canada   M4W 1K4

SALES DISTRIBUTION:
McArthur & Company
c/o Harper Collins
1995 Markham Road
Toronto, ON
M1B 5M8
toll free:
1 800 387 0117
1 800 668 5788 (fax)

Layout and Design by *MICHAEL P. CALLAGHAN*
Composed and Typeset at *MOONS OF JUPITER*, Toronto
Photographs by *JOHN MCCOMBE REYNOLDS*
Printed and Bound by *MARC VEILLEUX IMPRIMEUR*, Quebec

The publisher wishes to acknowledge
the assistance toward publication of the Canada Council
and the Ontario Arts Council.

The Canada Council
Conseil des Arts du Canada

ISBN 1-55096-547-6

Introduction: The Later Years

Rosemary Sullivan

*B*y the age of thirty-five, when the first poems in this volume were published, Gwendolyn MacEwen could already look back at a varied and complex career. A genuine autodidact (she left school at the age of eighteen before completing her high school matriculation), she had taught herself Hebrew, Arabic, Greek, and French, and had translated the works of writers in each of the four languages. She had travelled to Egypt, Israel, and Greece, published seven books of poetry, and two novels, including *King of Egypt, King of Dreams* which she had hoped would catapult her into the ranks of international historical novelists. She had written plays and seen them produced, including translations from classical Greek and a science fiction drama, *The World of Neshiah*, which was translated into Serbo-Croatian and broadcast on Trieste radio. She had published a collection of short stories, written programs for the CBC on Melville, Agatha Christie, the Song of Solomon, the Celebration of Evil, and also a story for children. Trained to play the violin in childhood, she wrote lyrics for a jazz cantata and provided the text for *Four Pieces for Baritone Voice and Orchestra* which would be performed by Victor Braun and orchestrated by Rudi van Dijk for the Toronto Symphony Orchestra. She had won prizes. She considered herself a professional writer, surviving as writers must, by her wits. "A poet doesn't have to be a myopic thing in an attic or a basement," she once wrote.

"He or she might well be a dynamic human being, truly involved in the gutsy aspects of life."

Her childhood, as Margaret Atwood has said, had determined her allegiances. Her mother's persistent mental illness (which she attributed to a British working-class childhood smashed by war, classism, and poverty) and her father's alcoholism made her believe modern life takes too many casualties. She had grown up in the atomic age of the sixties with the Vietnam war and many other small wars as backdrop. Her solitary travels to a divided Jerusalem in 1962 at the age of twenty-one, and later to Egypt in 1966, made her believe profoundly that we have to reinvent what it means to be human. That led to the visionary strain in her poetry, if one can use that over-worked term, and if by using it one means that she offered a critique, political, social, moral, and metaphysical, of modern society. Placing so little value on the imagination and the spirit, we were inevitably suffering the consequences.

But it was as a poet that MacEwen was best known. At twenty-one, after travelling through Israel, she decided, though she knew she was still "embryonic," that she could be a voice for her generation. Yet, in many ways one could say that the culture to which she spoke wasn't ready for her. She was, to use a clumsy term, an international nationalist before her time. Those who watched her forays into Mediterranean cultures thought she was simply pursuing the exotic, as an escapist might. But it was much more complex than that. She, so deeply read in politics and history, didn't believe in time. She wasn't particularly confident that human time meant much in the geological scale of things. "We *are* our ancestors," she wrote. "A lot of my images were centred on ancient civilizations simply because I am interested in the roots of things. I am interested in human history and how, in fact, we as modern people are very similar to our ancestors. We haven't changed all that much." She believed that there is a language of poetry that one has to learn, as one learns the language of the computer or the language of music. What was called the "archaic" or even primitive imagination of ancient civilizations seemed to match her own and she turned to them in quest of the myth and symbols she needed for her poetic searches. She believed the human imagination was of a piece. "Reality is an overwhelming thing for me. Every day for me is an overwhelming experience which requires continual analysis and understanding, and I can only understand reality in terms of this vast complex of mythological images and psychological truths." When asked if she had a "mythic imagination" she would reply: "Of course, what other kind is there? 'Myth' is a word we use to describe a sort of bridge between the so-called 'real' world and the world of the psyche. And of course for the poet the two are one."

She took the same approach to Canada. She saw it differently. It was a polytheistic culture, full of narratives to be written. She had invented a character called Noman (the name came not only from the voyaging Odysseus but from the noman's land that was the neutral territory in the borders of war) who was offered as the archetypal Canadian, amnesiac, multilingual, mythical, searching for the narrative of his country. Few poets found the resonances she did in Canadian landscape, writing of Grey Owl, Mackenzie King, or the doomed Franklin expedition to find the Northwest Passage. "I have found that this country is just as exotic as any other country. In fact, if anything, maybe even more mysterious."

She had a number of favorite metaphors, image pools on which she drew. Magicians and escape artists were one. "Poets are magicians without quick wrists," she said. The magician was a metaphor, of course, for the artist shifting the mind's hard shadows, the heavy twisted rocks of our thoughts. Like any poet she knew that the exciting territory was *inside*. If magicians worked in visual parables on the knife edge between reality and illusion, poetry was verbal parables: Poets "push at reality and come at it from the other side," she said. Appetite was another metaphor: "Eat," she would say. How can you comprehend anything without a tremendous desire, a tremendous appetite? At moments, she believed the cosmos fits. But there was another metaphor that seemed equally convincing. It was the desert — she saw it sometimes in the lonely wastes of a Canadian wilderness of snow, and in the bleak lunar landscapes of our minds. It also explained her attachment to Arabic cultures.

In 1982, she found her greatest strength yet in her T.E. Lawrence poems. Lawrence was for her a complex and lifelong obsession. She had read *Seven Pillars of Wisdom* as a teenager. In Israel she had encountered an Arab who had ridden with Lawrence. She claimed a family connection — her aunt Maud and a girlfriend whose diamond-dealing family met the Lawrences socially, visited T. E. ("Ned") at Clouds Hill in Dorset, and stayed overnight in the cottage. He had been gentle and considerate to the young ladies. MacEwen even impersonated Lawrence: I encountered a photograph of her on the Greek island of Antiparos, wearing a burnous, laughingly calling herself "Lawrence of Antiparos." She saw him as her twin, her male muse, another "Dreamer of the Day," haunting his own deserts. He was, she believed, a failed mystic. She had read Lawrence's own rather bad poems, but the long metric line in which he worked gave her the clue to the rhythm of her own poems and she wrote her stunning sequence.

Her last book *Afterworlds* seems to offer an uncanny sense of looking back and summing up. No doubt, this is a delusion simply because we know it was her last. In "Letters to Josef in Jerusalem" she writes to an Israeli friend from her youth whom she hasn't seen in twenty-five years, about the war that had continued uninterrupted for three decades. She returns to scenes of childhood, old lovers. The poems are apocalyptic. In "The Death of the Loch Ness Monster," she takes the perspective of the monster, "tired of pondering the possible existence of man." But the poems are also affirmations. She leaves us with what would prove to be her last word:

> *I hurl*
> *Breathless poems against my lord Death, send these*
> *words, these words*
> *Careening into the beautiful darkness.*

Gwendolyn MacEwen died November 30th, 1987, of a suspected heart attack brought on by excessive alcohol. It took a great deal of stamina to be Gwendolyn and she had run out of stamina.

She was in some strange way an archetype. Her extraordinary talent continues to speak not only in her own works, but in the works of her contemporaries. In Timothy Findley's novel *Headhunter*, she is disguised as the poet Amy, the model of the civilized human being. A small anthology could be made of the poems written about her. In her poem "Lines from Gwen; Lines for Ben," Phyllis Webb writes: "Why was it we who were magic animals could not fit into poems and be happy?" But it is not an age in which a poet can be happy if, as Gwendolyn did, she sees too well.

Gwendolyn MacEwen

VOLUME TWO

The Later Years

From KING OF EGYPT, KING OF DREAMS

Gwendolyn MacEwen began work on her historical novel about the life of the heretic Pharaoh, Akhenaton, in 1965. It would preoccupy her until it was published by Macmillan in 1971. Akhenaton fascinated MacEwen. During his brief reign from 1377 to 1360 B.C., the Pharaoh devoted his life to propagating his new religion, Atonism, based on the worship of a single God whose divinity lay in the vital and omnipresent energy of the sun. While he concentrated on expunging the worship of other gods, the once great Egyptian empire collapsed, reduced to little more than a nation state. In the historical record Akhenaton is credited with having precociously "invented" the idea of monotheism.

The section from MacEwen's novel reprinted here is the last chapter, the fictional "papyrus" of Meritaton, daughter of Akhenaton, in which she speaks of her dead husband, Smenkhare, whom Akhenaton had made his co-regent at the end of his reign. MacEwen speculates that Smenkhare is Meritaton's brother. His reign was brief. He was murdered, she suggests, by a vengeful priestly caste bent on destroying Akhenaton's heretical legacy, and replaced on the throne by his brother Tutankhamen. This is the prose equivalent of the poetic sequence, *The Nine Arcana of the Kings*, which concludes volume one of *The Poetry of Gwendolyn MacEwen*.

THE PAPYRUS OF MERITATION
Circa 1349 B.C.

Give me the hands that hold your soul
And I will receive your soul and never die.
Call upon me by name and forever and ever
And never shall it sound without reply.

No, Smenkhare, I told no one where I buried you. Would the Nile ever reveal its source? Often from out of the dark deserts of my sleep I cry *"lfnai, lfnai, he is mine!"* for in death you are mine as in my own death I am yours.

It is easy to die, easier than I ever would have thought. I simply do not eat; I let my body consume itself bit by bit and burn itself out like a candle. They cannot deny me this privilege; I am a royal person and my last command is to be allowed to die. Oh, there are some who try to talk me out of it — my sister Ankhesenamon, who is queen, and my grandfather, the Vizier Ay. He comes almost every day and pleads with me, but I spit on him, this "Priest of Maat." His face is dark and sullen like the bottom of a pool; his eyes are slanted and his mouth curls downward in a perpetual sneer. I sense there is blood on his hands, but I don't know whose. Sometimes I think it is our father's blood. Today I slapped his mouth (I hate his mouth) and he left my room with his head hanging, like a sick dog.

Tutankhamon struts about his palace in a robe studded with little golden rosettes, playing at his newest game of being king. The Horizon is no more and the royal house dwells once again in the city of Amon. After his coronation the little beast took his revenge upon you, and permitted the priests to close down your mortuary temple and forbid you the privileges of a royal burial. He, like them, did not acknowledge that you were ever king. The servants of Amon confiscated all you possessed; they seized the three golden shrines that were to house your coffin, the little golden coffins for your vital organs, the chairs and couches, the *ka-house* for your statue — everything. They ground out your name from the furnishings and one day they will be used for the tomb of Tutankhamon. May it be soon! May he meet his death in some disgusting ignoble manner that will make people snicker and laugh!

Meanwhile your body lies in the dankest, filthiest hole in the Valley of the West; even a peasant would shun it as his final house, but in your meagre death, Smenkhare, you are more of a king than the spoiled boy who now sits on the throne.

I feel I am eight years old again, and I am falling, falling onto the magical floor in the palace of the Horizon. My big turquoise ball rolls across the pavement, over the animals and birds, the painted cranes standing one-legged in their painted marshes. It rolls over the flat papyrus thickets, the herons and flamingos and kingfishers and ducks. How I loved that floor — the green zigzags on the plaster, the tall reeds and flat faces of the captives of Khor! I used to sit in the different squares and make fantasies about the occupants. One day I was in the papyrus thicket square, which in itself was not very exciting, but it reminded me of the times my nurse Benremut took me to the river bank to play among the waterplants, dozing there and having horrible dreams of the ovens of Hell, the lakes of Fire, the Swallowers. Dreams of crocodiles surfacing from the water with the hands of Horus between their teeth — the most honorable death was to fall into the Nile and be devoured by a crocodile — dreams of Isis hovering in the air like a hawk over the corpse of Osiris, taking his seed. I didn't know what that last part meant, but it sounded wonderful, and after all, I couldn't understand all the legends Benremut told me. Father said I had to forget those awful tales, for they had no part in the Teaching. He told Benremut to shut her mouth, which was hard on her, for her mouth was all she had, really. She was never quite the same afterwards; she'd sit all day stringing collars and cursing when she dropped the beads. She'd learned the curses from Ay, who was always willing to share his vocabulary with anybody who was interested.

She couldn't care less about the floor. I couldn't understand how anybody could just walk over it to get somewhere, without getting lost in it, or lying flat out upon it like I did. Flat out, my toes stretching far as the foot of the flamingo, my fingers reaching back to poke out the eye of the Khorian.

I was the Beloved of Aton, and I wore long strands of jewels in my ears and a wide collar of flowers and nothing else. My fingernails were bright silver, and all the hair was shaven from my head except for one sidelock held by a turquoise ring. This drew attention to my long narrow head. All my sisters had long heads too, like our father; he permitted us to wear no headdresses to disguise the elongation of our skulls. It was not an abnormality, he said, but a sign.

I was small and tubular and unripe, and my body was for me a kind of toy, a lithe nut-brown thing with no dark places, no secrets.

The big turquoise ball went plop into the pond and I lay back imagining that I was painted onto the floor. Father would come and be unable to find me; he'd walk all over me and I'd just scream with laughter. Then he'd look down and see that his princess no longer lived in the world of men. They'd bring me my food and I'd still have to continue my writing lessons, but it would all be so much more tolerable. How silly everyone would look — giving advice to the floor, scolding it, taking orders from it! I laughed out loud and Benremut looked up dully. Like her father Ay, she had no sense of humor. She never smiled. She laughed a lot, but that's different.

Then I looked up and saw you standing in the doorway. You were brown and lean and you wore the pleated linen tunic of a young aristocrat. You were confident but not arrogant; you seemed overly serious, always brooding over some secret problem. But you were only eleven then, and the sidelock hadn't yet been shaven from your head. Your eyes were wonderfully clear and large, your features small but well shaped. And your teeth, when I could see them on the rare occasions of your laughter, were even and white. You were so restrained and controlled, but there were always parts of your body which betrayed you — a flickering muscle in the cheek, a hand clenching and unclenching. Your left eye, more candid and clear than your right . . .

You stood for a moment absorbed in something, then wandered over to me and sat down on the Khorian's left foot. A small live bird was pulsating in your palm and you held it out to me. "I caught it this morning in the marshes, do you want to hold it?" you asked. I answered, "I'm a floor, and a floor can't hold anything!" but then I felt rather silly and accepted the tiny throbbing bundle of white feathers. You showed me your new throwstick, painted bright blue and decorated with flowers and *Wedjet* eyes. "The king your father gave it to me, it's the same kind as his!" you said proudly. "When I throw it, it's so well glazed that it catches the light and flies like a shiny blue hawk against the sky!" You fondled the weapon and I watched you, proud that you chose to speak to me about such remote boy's business.

"I just clipped this bird on the wing, enough for it to fall," you said, and while its warm vibrant belly nestled in my palm I told you about my father's aviary which was going to be built in the North Palace with hundreds of little niches for nests and long drinking troughs. I asked if you intended giving him the bird, and you replied very emphatically that you'd catch a rare one for him — one he could never find himself. At that moment you reminded me of someone I knew very well, so well that it was impossible to recall.

You looked down at my body. "You have no breasts," you said.

Now I had often watched how grown-up ladies behaved with men, and I replied with what I thought was the proper mixture of coyness and sophistication. True, I was only eight, but in Keme one learns such things very early. "In three years my breasts will start growing, I was told they would. But if you speak to me again about breasts I'll tell Benremut. You may come back in three years and see them, though — if you like." Then I turned sideways and pressed my fists down between my legs in what I thought was an attitude of mature indignation. "You don't have any either!" I cried.

"But I don't want any."

"You have *something else*, and I know all about it."

"And that's another thing you don't have!"

"I don't need one — so there!"

"Well, you look pretty funny without it," you said, staring down at the naked little hump between my legs.

I took the bird and placed it there, to cover my nakedness, but you gently removed it from my lap and held it by the feet while it fluttered and tested its wings.

"When you have breasts," you whispered, "I will come and touch them."

I started to protest but when I saw your mouth pulled back in a wide flashing grin, I forgot what I was going to say and gazed fascinated at the most beautiful teeth I had ever seen. Nevertheless, I vowed to tell my father of your impertinence.

"Keep the bird," you said, "and in three years it will fly away free." You forced it back into my hands, got up from the floor, and passed out through the gates. The blue throwstick still flashed in your hands, catching the afternoon rays of the Aton on its glaze. I stayed a while longer and tried to renew my games, but soon lost interest and found myself musing on how the north harem where you lived was almost exactly opposite my quarters in the royal estate, across the Royal Road. And from the top terrace of my father's garden, where all the trees were, it would be very easy to see.

Then suddenly I was ten, and I watched Father's artisans make my set of coffins. Strange to be a child and look dispassionately upon one's own house of death. Foreigners think that we in the Two Lands love death, but how wrong they are! We hate it and dread it and we furnish ourselves for the great journey well in advance. It is life we love, jealously, painfully, and wish to continue it forever.

They were grinding up lumps of red ochre into a paint crimson as blood. There were three coffins — each to be contained in the other, like three generations, I think; past, present, and future. The middle one was made of wood and covered with great sheets of gold foil inlaid with a feather pattern of turquoise and carnelian stones. A long strip of gold ran from the chest to the feet, awaiting the insertion of the signs which would identify me. I watched them lay the gold mask over the wooden face and I stood transfixed with its beauty and wished my own face could be pure gold.

Then I felt something behind me, and turned to see you watching me, your head cocked at a studious angle, your eyes slightly squinting. "I am thirteen today," you announced, and stared at the coffin with its great wings of jewels. You walked around it, your face clouded with some strange trouble.

"What's wrong, don't you like it?" I asked.

"I don't know, don't ask. I think I saw a name on the golden strip."

"My name will be on it, and my father's, and the name of the Aton."

"Those were not the names I saw," you said.

We walked down the long path from the palace to the river and the way was lined with shrubs and palms. Father's barge floated on the green water held by mooring stakes to the shore; its dozens of oars languished in the river like tongues, its masts were straight as young men's spines, white sails shivered high above the bright red cabin. Around it were sycamore skiffs, single-sailed boats, a few freight ships waiting to carry out their cargoes of colored glass which the Horizon manufactured. Fishermen, their faces brown as ancient papyrus, sat mending nets by the shore.

"You still have no breasts, Beloved."

"Next year I will. This year I have buds and they hurt me."

"I bet you can't run, then. I've seen girls your age running and they look like they're going to fall apart."

"I can run!" I cried, and to prove it I darted down to the river bank and collapsed beneath a palm. You sat beside me and drew up your knees to your chin and rocked back and forth. We spoke of the seasons and you told me your favorite month was this one, Hathor, because it was your birthday, because the river receded and the air cooled and the peasants sowed their crops. I told you mine was the first month of the flood, and you replied that that was how it should be, for the river in its inundation was like a woman, while the river receding lean and calm was more like a man. I didn't see the point, but I nodded wisely and told you about the time I found a foreign coin left behind by the Nile; I had washed the mud from it and shown it to my father. But he had thrown it back into the Nile, for there was an image on it which displeased him.

Once again an expression came over your face which reminded me of someone I knew very well.

"What are all your other names?" I asked.

"Names! I have a hundred names!" and then you recited something:

In the Great House and in the House of Fire
On the dark night of the counting of all the years,
On the dark night when months and years are numbered,
O let my name be given back to me!

I asked you what it meant but you said you really didn't know. You found it written in one of the ancient books in the Baou Ra.

"But the books in the Baou Ra libraries are forbidden!" I cried.

"Not to me they aren't," you murmured, and your expression told me the matter was closed.

We watched the green heaving river for a long time. The great Nile with its seven mouths, its living pulse, its green death. We argued about its source, for I believed it was born in the Underworld, but you scoffed and called me a child. You had known that was untrue, since the tender age of seven, and since then had lacked all such illusions. You several times got into fist-fights with your young friends over it.

"All right, then, where *is* the source?" I asked.

"What do you mean, where is the source? I don't know *that*. I only know it's *a secret of movement, a darkness in daytime*. Wanre told me that."

You were silent a long while, then said suddenly, "Would you like to live long?"

"Father says the Aton determines the length of life. And you?"

"Short, like the wind. I want to burn and die like a thunderbolt, like a flame."

The living river was west; the hollow tombs in the cliffs were east. Between life and death we sat, between the water and the stone we sat, children who did not know the meaning of our own words. We went back to the palace and parted at the gates.

"I understand nothing," you said, and I burst into a fit of nervous laughter (I'd been laughing a lot lately; it had something to do with having hurting buds of breasts and being almost eleven). Then I ran away and left you standing alone. Now when I think of you I do not remember you as a king, but as a boy on his thirteenth birthday saying, "*I understand nothing.*" And I did not even know the nothing which you didn't understand.

I remember the day I wore a necklace of glass fish and grasshoppers joined by small glass suns, and a palm-leaf basket laughing with flowers hung from my arm. The air was a web of gold as we walked through the gardens of the summer palace of Meru Aton. Ahead of us was my private shrine, surrounded by tiny canals and water-plants, and I told you that yesterday I'd offered a goose and five ripe melons to the god. You trailed along with me beside the gurgling musical canals and said that my father's world was a miniature garden like this one, and that he must begin to look outside, or the weeds would eat their way into his world and destroy it.

"That's monstrous!" I cried. "If you were king, what would you do?"

"I'd preserve the garden," you said, "I'd make terms with the weeds!"

Just then I spotted a rabbit and went bounding after it behind a bush. I got down on my belly and tried to poke my arm through the little thicket where I saw it disappear, but it got away. I felt you drop softly beside me then.

"Princess, you have breasts. Let me touch them!"

"But Benremut —"

"Is busy watching her reflection in the water . . . "

Shyly you placed your hand on one breast, then on another. You touched a glass fish on my collar and said you wished you were a fish plunging and dipping into mysterious rivers or swimming about in secret enchanted pools. Just then your finger caught on one of the grasshopper's sharp glass feet and you winced with pain. A drop of blood appeared at the tip. I rolled over and over on the grass laughing at you, but suddenly your young body was flat upon me and your mouth covered my mouth. For a moment I did not breathe or move; then I pushed you away. "She's coming!" I whispered. And we had just enough time to get up from the grass before Benremut reached us.

That night, alone, I caressed the small glass fish. I wanted to touch that secret part of you I'd never seen but only felt when you were upon me, that strong hard part between your legs which was made to dive and swim in dark unknown rivers. Recently my mother had told me I should expect something very soon. She had wept, and I had asked myself, why was Nefertiti weeping, she who was so beautiful, no one in the whole kingdom was half so beautiful, why did my mother weep?

And a week after you fell upon me beneath the bushes of Meru Aton, the red wetness between my thighs told me I had become a woman. The kiss must have made it begin in me, your hard body must have drawn it out.

A month before you became my husband we couldn't encounter each other without stammering and blushing, for the memory of that afternoon in the summer palace loomed up before us golden and red. Now you were eighteen, and I, fifteen. Tiy was dead. My beautiful mother Nefertiti was dead. We were no more children. We knew more was to come for us than a kiss in the bushes or a cut finger from the edge of a glass grasshopper. What would it be like? I asked myself a thousand times but my imagination called up only the most hazy pictures. Behind the haze, though, my blood coursed strong as the Nile in flood, and my blood knew. It would be a new and secret form of night. The Lord of the Atmosphere holds heaven and earth apart, but when Nut descends to lie with Geb, everything becomes dark as it was in the beginning.

On our wedding night after the feasts and dances were over, we were alone in our vast apartments. Two great eunuchs stood in the hall outside our door, guarding, not our privacy as I then thought, but our very lives. I turned upon you, forgetting everything but the gnawing doubts in my mind, and demanded to know your plans once you were on the throne. Were the ugly rumors true? Would you tear down all that Father had built? Would you use him like the others had? I was white with anger, but you remained very quiet, letting me circle around you, listening and not listening.

"Sister . . ." you said.

"I don't want any romantic words from you!" I cried. But I saw that flashing smile on your face, the one I'd seen years ago when you brought me a bird you'd caught in the marshes.

"Let me tell you something . . ." you began, but I strode across the room, carefully avoiding the sumptuous bed strewn with flowers and sprinkled with a dozen different scents.

"Don't come any nearer . . . upstart!" I cried, and you followed me with your hand held out, smiling still, making a game of my anger. Then I trembled, for something delicate was moving within me, something raw and untouched.

"I'm not going to destroy the king," you said. "I'm going to restore him. What do you think he and I have been talking about these last four years? Now . . . look in my eyes, Beloved of Aton, and tell me who I remind you of . . . "

I looked and my hand flew to my mouth in surprise. The same narrow eyes, the same features, only softer, saner than his. Why had I not seen it before?

"Now you know why I call you *sister*. Once he asked me whose blood flowed in my veins, and was it the blood of Amenhotep. And I said 'No,' feeling at that moment something touch me soft and sharp as a wish. 'No,' I said . . . and I whispered, *'Royal brother, yours!'* but his back was turned. Look, my mother Sitamon was his sister, and he lay with her — I know this, for he told me — when he was a boy no older than I. He doesn't really know if I am his . . . but he's watched me all these years. He called me the Child of the Aton, he called me his Beloved. Today he called me *his son*."

"Who else knows?" I asked, my voice so soft I could scarcely hear it.

"No one. He says it would mean my death to have it known."

Now I looked at you and whispered *"brother,"* and the word was not strange on my tongue; it was as though I had spoken it inwardly a thousand times. We stared at each other and saw nothing but the shadow of the king our father who had made us one. Your flesh was my flesh; your mouth, my mouth. The great wings of the royal hawk thrashed the air between us. You took my hand in yours and placed it over your hard sex as once many years before you gave me the white wild bird you caught, to hold, to feel its shape and pulse, that I might not fear it.

"I don't want to hurt you, sister . . . "

"It will only be the first moment."

Then we were sinking into the vast bed of linen and flowers, into a private garden, into the magical painted floor of the palace to lose ourselves among the birds and lotuses. And we were lost among the magic squares, we were children lost in the bushes of Meru Aton, we were man and woman lost in the great bed which had become the world.

And I murmured from the depths of the garden, "Come down, my brother, come down." And you came and roughly ripped the collar of beads and flowers from my throat and threw it across the room where it fell in a hundred pieces. We watched each other's faces and smiled; we were on the verge of laughter, triumphant silver laughter of children no more children. Our eyes never closed, not once, as the profound flowers pulled us down and down. And when our bodies came together it was heaven descending upon earth and creating night. My loins rose and called you in, and the pain was a moment felt and forgotten like the pain the glass grasshopper once gave your finger. My body obeyed some instinct it never knew it possessed. It swam, it danced. It arched up once, and again — and the movement surprised you and you gasped, and the gates of your loins opened. And as the sweet salt seed burst from your sex another instinct made me open my mouth wide with a cry or a laugh —

"O my brother, yes, *yes!* "

The next morning your soul, like a new alien body, throbbed within mine. And across the room was a sea of beads from my broken collar.

The day we left the Horizon the quays were crowded with vessels flying bright ribbons and streamers; hundreds of masts rose from the river and the shores were lined with silent citizens waving limp flowers and palm leaves. From the west gate of the palace a long line of porters and officials came to follow us down the flowered path to the river. It was the same path we had walked as children, but now we were the co-rulers of Keme. Would we ever walk down that path again?

The silence of the crowds on the shoreline filled me with fear and the faces of the officials were drawn and tense. Father waited for us, motionless beneath a red and blue canopy, clutching the royal emblems to his breast as though he feared someone would take them away if he held them less tightly. Then you and he faced each other for the last time, and your eyes searched one another's eyes for a reassurance neither could give. There was nothing to say. You wore the Blue Crown, the helmet of war, the crown he had worn in his youth.

And when I embraced him his body felt like some great shivering plant that the merest wind could destroy.

The great boats pulled away from the shore and formed a long procession in the river. But the silence on the banks was the silence of a funeral, and I felt we were sailing upstream towards the Valley of Death in a blaze of boats, and that we were already dead.

I looked back and saw that the red and blue canopy had become a purple splash in the distance. I imagined him under it, still clutching the royal emblems, his knuckles dead white from the strain, a small river of blood running down his wrist. I screamed with fear and ran into the cabin, and you came and hid your head in my breast and whispered, "I know, I feel it too. Time closing in on us, *myriads of years*, a string of endless suns hanging about our necks. We are the land. Last night I was strong, I dreamed I was Horus the Avenger, plucking out my eye to save my father. I whispered, *I come to thee, Father, arise for me. I gather thy bones, I make thee whole . . .* but today I am weak. I feel him there, downstream. I feel we will not see him again!"

"Say no more!" I cried, and held you to me. We clung to each other because we were more than ourselves; we were *him*, we were his body, his blood, and in our embrace we held him together, and in our separation he fell apart. And only when we loved was he made whole.

For most of the journey we stayed in the cabin. Neither of us wanted to look at the river.

Do you remember the incredible old hag who came in front of our procession in the city of Amon, who stood before our litter and refused to give way? She traced a circle in the sand with one naked hideous foot and mumbled something under her breath. One of the guards stepped forward to remove her, but on seeing her face he winced and moved away. She screeched like an owl and came up beside you and bent her head down to yours and whispered something in your ear. I never learned what she said, you would never tell me . . . but the power of her words could be seen in the sudden pallor which drained your face. You drew back, your mouth taut; your hand flew to the insignia of the god which hung from your collar. The hag laughed and disappeared into the crowd.

And our scribe Pawah identified her. "*That,*" he said, "was the Divine Consort of Amon in the days of Amenhotep. That bundle of rags was once the High Priestess of Opet!"

I trembled with cold. I had heard that her power had been great. That gruesome witch with the filthy breath had once lain with the god Amenhotep as the earthly wife of Amon, and had wielded as much influence as the High Priest himself. It was said that hers was the voice of the oracle which had first cursed our father when he was a child. Today she had cursed you. I begged you to tell me what she had said, but your lips tightened, and the chill in my bones sank deeper.

And when we entered the gates of the palace of Amenhotep you remarked that it looked like the dry bones of a desert bird picked clean by vultures. I could not bring myself to believe that I had been born within those walls. The peaks of the West rose up beyond them, and it was as though we had already entered the land of death.

In those horrible months at the old capital there was one thing which frightened me more than the chaos which surrounded us. I did not conceive. Your seed did not take root in me. The simplest peasant could lie with his woman once in the fields and she'd become fertile, but though we lay together a hundred times I was empty. Was that the curse the witch placed upon you? I wept into the hollow place between your shoulder and collarbone and cried that the gods were taking their revenge on our father by making us sterile. You tried to soothe me with silly jokes and puns (*remyet, romyet*, man was made from the tears of the Creator) — but even as you did your own body trembled and we made love in furious, frightened defiance of whatever perverse force choked the life in our loins. I took to wearing a knotted cord around my neck as a charm — the kind that peasants use — made of small cowrie shells which looked like the vulva of a woman.

Then one night I dreamed I saw you slain on the altar of the sun, and the next morning I feared for you and took Pawah with me and went into the temple of Ra-Horakhte. I found you as in the dream, fallen across the altar. The gates of heaven broke and the great vaults collapsed around me. The universe burst in my head and the body of Nut with its flesh of stars was soaked red with your blood. Your face was turned down, as though in the shame of your own death, and you were one with the sacrifices. The Blue Crown lay at your feet. I bent over you and called your name.

Pawah went into the dark recesses of the shrine and sought out a servant and asked, "*Who did it?*" And the fool answered with a smirk, "Ask not who is guilty, but who is *innocent* these days, O scribe of Ankheprure!" Then your gentle Pawah struck the man across the mouth.

And when we went to take you away, my brother, the altar of the sun burned with its offerings and you lay among the bloody flowers and the bread.

The same day word came of the death of our father. I do not remember anything about the weeks that followed. I think perhaps I became Isis and kept watch over your body for endless days.

By the time your body was ready for burial Tutankhamon was already on the throne and your belongings had been seized. There was only one place to bury you — the filthy hole where the desecrators had thrown the shrine of Tiy. I cringed to think that such a foul place would be your house of death, but there was nowhere else.

We gathered together all we could find — cast-off bits of things in the palace, discarded pieces of furniture made for others. I felt as though I was combing the world for those miserable trinkets which would accompany you on your journey. Then the meagre furnishings assumed gigantic proportions in my imagination. I listed in my mind again and again the articles which would surround you, as though the repetition of the list would somehow increase their number. Even now it soothes me to remember them:

— Four magical bricks bearing the name our father bore when he first took the throne. We feared to insert your name in place of his, lest they crumble to dust.

— Four alabaster jars made for me when I was a girl, to contain my vital organs when I died. They had my portrait on the lids, and the irises of the eyes were black jasper. I had glass cobras added to the brows, and my name ground away from the surface of the jars.

— One small trinket box containing an inner box full of broken, useless things — small vases and playing wands and pendants of ibises, and a little silver goose head . . .

— And one of the coffins father had made for me in the City of the Horizon. (Remember the day you stood behind me watching the artists work upon it? You saw a name and it made you afraid; now I know it was your own name you saw.) It was the middle coffin in the set of three, and we changed it from that of a princess to that of a king. It was as though my own body was being reworked to accommodate your death. My golden hands holding *ankhs* became your hands clutching the royal emblems — a crook and a flail of blue glass beads on rods of bronze. The gold mask which was my face became your face; a blue beard was added, and a green and gold cobra on the brow. The words on the strips which were to have run down my body were changed from feminine to royal male, and down the length of the coffin from chest to foot the brilliant red and blue letters were adjusted to spell your name: *"Beloved of the King of the Upper and*

Lower Land who lives in Truth, Lord of the Two Lands, the
goodly child of the living Aton, who lives forever and ever,
Smenkhare."

It took the workers from twilight to dawn to drag the poor furnishings down the stairs into the shabby hole and arrange your house of death. We paid them well, but they never knew who they were burying. When first we led them through the dark Valley they were quiet, but when they saw where we were going they let up shrieks and groans and vowed they would approach no closer the dirty little tomb where the desecrators had thrown Tiy's shrine. A serpent dwelled within it, they said, with eyes that could paralyse a man and render him mad and impotent for the rest of his days.

Then with one great sweeping gesture Pawah lifted the sheet from your coffin and pointed to the royal cobra on the brow whose eyes gleamed in the moonlight. "There is yet another serpent whose gaze can paralyse a man!" he cried. And as they shrank back in fear he shouted, "Choose!" They chose, and continued their work.

But during the night it required more gold to hold them to their task, for one of them kept scaring his companions out of their wits by pointing to moving shadows on the tomb walls or claiming that the coffin lid had burst open of its own accord, or by stepping over the collapsed walls of Tiy's shrine with his feet making a noise like that of a barking dog against the thin metal. The night was filled with their prayers to Amon and Ptah and Hathor until they had called down the entire colony of the gods to protect them in their deed. Once one of the men, who was very drunk, fell down trembling and begged to be allowed to go home, but at that very moment the others accidentally banged the coffin against the shrine, and he took it as a sign of royal anger. Green-faced and gasping, he went about his work.

When it was over, I stood alone in the tomb, aware for the first time of the peeling plaster and the reeking dampness of the walls. An old leak near the door had been cemented over once in the past, but now it opened again, and a trickle of water crawled along the floor towards the lion-headed bier which supported your coffin. One drop per hour, maybe more, maybe less, would flow beneath your body. One drop per hour for eternity . . . enough to rot the bier, the coffin, and all its contents! There was no time now to shift you to the eastern wall. How many years until those drops attack the wood of the bier, then soak through and soften the linen strips which bind you . . . and then seep into your flesh?

I put my fist to my mouth to stop the scream. I removed the white sheet from the coffin and in the half-light from the torches I saw something else. There was a thin line of shadow along the side where the lid had slipped open from rough handling. That child's coffin was too small for a man . . . and some of the gilt plating had been knocked off from the foot-end when it had lurched and bumped down the stairs of the shaft.

I heard an argument going on outside; the burial crew was threatening to return home without sealing up the tomb unless their payment was doubled. Pawah's angry words echoed down the shaft. "Scum! Drunkards and death-mongers! You've been paid enough. Scavengers — you would turn around and break open this same tomb tomorrow if there was enough wealth in it. But I warn you this place is doubly cursed!"

There was a silence and I heard Pawah lower his voice and invent a last cunning story to scare them off. "Do you know who you've buried this night?" he asked.

And into the uncomprehending silence which followed he flung the words, "You've buried the bones of Tiy, who was a commoner like yourselves and whose body was destroyed on the pyres of the desecrators!"

They fell at the mouth of the tomb blubbering with horror. Not one of them would reveal the whereabouts of the place, not now.

I stood over you. All the torches had flickered out save one, and its light played upon your golden mask, your hands. I suddenly remembered that of the three coffins — past, present, and future — this was the middle one, the present. Only it had survived, for the past was destroyed and the future unsown. Inside it you lay with one of my collars about your neck and three of my bracelets on each of your arms. Your fingers were capped with little caps of gold; once your living fingers upon me had been warm as the sun. And you were crowned, for days before I had torn the golden vulture from your chest and twisted it round and round and placed it on your head.

You lay in the attitude of a woman as we had arranged you — left arm across the chest, right arm straight down with the hand against the thigh, to mislead anyone who might one day find you and think you were the Beloved of the Criminal.

I knelt at your feet and read the prayer which was cut into the gold foil:

> *I breathe the sweet air from your mouth*
> *And gaze upon your beauty every day.*
> *To hear your voice like the north wind*
> *Is all I pray,*
> *For love will give life to my bones.*

Give me the hands that hold your soul
And I will receive your soul and never die.
Call upon me by name forever and ever
And never shall it sound without reply.

Then I heard myself crying *"Smenkhare!,"* the syllables
bursting upon the foul air of the tomb, their sweetness for
a moment erasing the salt smell of death. *"Smenkhare,
Smenkhare!"* . . . remembering the time when as children
we had run laughing to the river bank, our feet tangled in
flowers and river-plants, the kiss in the bushes of Meru
Aton, the drop of blood on your finger from the glass
ornament. I had laughed then, to see your blood. And in
my mind an old song:

O fair boy, come to your house,
I am your sister whom you love,
You cannot leave me
My brother, my brother!

. . . The bed of ebony and straw, our bodies strain-
ing the woven cord beneath us, my necklace of cowrie
shells clattering and protesting in our dance of love. . .

"The dawn!" Pawah shouted from the top of the
shaft.

I did not answer, for there was one thing left to do.
Now I was unreal, yet fully real. It did not seem strange
to me when I found myself hovering over you like Isis
hovered over Osiris in the form of a hawk. Nor when I
felt myself lying along you, the length of my body along
the full length of the gold and turquoise and carnelian let-
ters, the brilliant signs which spelled your name. Then the
name was burned into my own flesh from breast to foot.
My arms were the wings of death embracing you, and it

seemed my loins received your last gift, the seed of your death.

Then I stepped over Tiy's shrine which still lay unhinged at the entrance. Banged up and beaten, it bore the titles of that fearful woman who was my grandmother. On the panel she and Father were making burnt offerings to the god; his image had been obliterated, yet the marks of its obliteration were deeper than the outlines of her body.

I went up the filthy stairs out of the tomb, and stepped out of the foul dampness of your eternal house and into the slanting rays of dawn. The workers re-sealed the tomb with the seal of the nine captives beneath the jackal, the symbol of the priestly college of Amon-Ra. The seal of the past had been broken only once, and then restored.

The rays of the Aton were remote, virginal. The power of the god was in its rawest form. Things were merely being *lit* by it, not drawn towards it. Was this the horror that my father had felt, was this his private fear — the *remoteness* of the god? There was nothing beneficial now in those awful rays, nor did it seem to me there was anything simple about dark and light — for this cold impersonal dawn was for me another kind of darkness, a new and secret form of night.

My life is as worthless now as a grain of chaff or a single bead. But I don't fear death. You lie within my own coffin, and it is like the shell of my body containing you forever. You are caressed by my great wings of red and blue and gold. My end is upon me, but it is my victory. *Smenkhare!* I possess your secret name; did you not grant me your eternal soul when you told it to me? O my brother, your breath is locked forever in my ears where once the name was whispered, and I defy eternity to take from me what is mine! . . . I have just remembered something. Before I left your tomb I pulled a single cowrie shell from my collar and placed it in the dirt at your feet. Your *ba* will see it glittering there forever like small brilliant vulva, the entrance and the exit of life. You will remember the curled and swirling passages of our love. *You will call upon me by name and never*

From **THE FIRE-EATERS**

> *We all have second-degree burns*
> *And they hurt but the hurt doesn't matter.*
>
> *The living flame of the world is what matters*

The Fire-Eaters was published by Oberon Press in 1976.

MacEwen usually organized her books of poems thematically. "I write a group of poems," she explained. "As I begin to understand what is the overriding concern in these poems, then I find my title, my theme, and I arrange my poems in such a way that they will congregate around the theme." Here the theme is the fire-eaters: the world is a living flame that we must consume and it is always painful. Most of the poems were composed during a particularly difficult stretch in her life when her second marriage was disintegrating. But even here MacEwen's characteristic self-mocking, sardonic humor is evident, as in her autobiographical sequence, "Animal Syllables," looking back at the time she lived on Ward's Island in Toronto harbor: "It seems I have one foot in one world and the other foot in another; I think I need new shoes." The sequence, "The Carnival," was written for a jazz cantata composed by Ron Collier and first performed by him in Detroit with Bruno Gerussi as narrator.

THE CARNIVAL

1

I danced before I learned to walk
And spoke before I learned to talk
I can do almost anything
But me myself I cannot sing.
Who am I, and who
Lives in the carnival behind my eye?

I swallow swords, I swallow fire
Twice a day for a very small fee
I am everyone's desire.
Do you know me?
I escape from ropes and chains
But I am not free, I am
The juggler juggling worlds behind your eye
I am the prisoner of me.

Who escapes from all the knots
The world can tie?
I swallow my words like swords
And cry
Who am I, and who
Lies in the carnival behind my eye?

2

I joined myself in the Mirror House
When all the children had gone home.
Hey! dancer, juggler, fire-eater, clown!
The crippled mirror stops you where you stand
The mirror has just stolen your left hand
And the whole glass house comes tumbling down.

I dance alone, I asked to dance alone
Inside the silver mirrors of my mind
Inside the living prison of my bones.

3

The wheel of the carnival turns forever
And I am its crazy seasonal rider.
I can't get off it, either
For when I paid my fare I said:
I want a ticket for the endless ferris
Let me on it, let me on!
And the man said: *It'll cost you plenty.*
And I answered:
I can't stand to see the great wheel empty,
Let me on it, let me on!
And he said: *Okay, man, it's your money.*

But it's funny because sometimes
I'm glad I can't get off it.
I circle, I rise, I fall.
I seem to move better than anyone below
Even though I can't move at all.

4

I danced before I learned to walk
And spoke before I learned to talk
I can do almost anything
But me myself I cannot sing.
Who am I, and who
Lives in the carnival behind my eye?

The singer who falls back into the song
The dancer who falls back into the dance
Houdini who falls back into his chains
To imprison himself again,
To laugh.
Who lives in the carnival which is you?
I do, I do.

5

Ladies and gentlemen I'll dance for you
Twice a day for a very small fee
Or I'll break chains and swallow fire
If you follow me.
I'll juggle worlds before your eyes
I am the way, I am the light.
Lock me up and I'll be free
To dance forever, if you follow me.

ANIMAL SYLLABLES

Let me say right off that this is no answer, for no question has as yet been posed. The gulls, merely, have gone mad out on the lake and have turned pure white for Christmas. Who has seen the future in retrospect? The lighthouse keeper at the end of the pier has nothing to say, and the great light rotates at the tip of the tower. The waves recur, the light, the seasons; memories flash and turn and guide the ships of wisdom in. I want to record the colors, the redness, the sea-green, the pure white; I want my syllables pure as the speech of gulls, or foxes.

The gulls are always screaming from the end of the long stone tongue which is the pier; the lake is always tasting the beach where once I lay beside the beachfire, my forehead facing Orion; the breakwater always chastises the waves, and the place where I pasted a poem with surf to a rock remains. It is earth, and surf, and blood; art is a small crime I commit against the seasons, or sometimes an elaborate lie my better sense rejoices in. And all the while the waves insist, present me with their patient, disciplined argument: *It has all been said before.*

The rocks talk, and the lighthouse describes Cabbalistic arcs all over the darkness. What color was I wearing in September when the beach turned infra-red a second before the sunset? A red sweater, I remember now, and I bent over a strange shell. I could see the veins of my hands beneath the flesh; a black steamer passed silently through the channel; the shameless sun streamed over my left shoulder and set. Everything seemed gentle, and wild; a single gull was the Holy Spirit, a savage dove; a white dog was the violent Lamb. Dark, I built a beachfire and thought about the flames and the earth. In the darkness I constructed a fire; in the midst of the fire I began to gather another darkness.

The two cats, Cagliostro and Sundog, are constantly repairing themselves, combing, pulling, licking; it's almost as if they are able to anticipate some sort of ultimate wound and heal it in advance. The waves take care of the rocks in the same way, although they wear away with so much attention. Do all the soothing tongues of mothers, and seas, and lovers melt and wear away the flesh and rock they seek to heal? Do we die thin from the thousand kisses that drive the hurt away?

Kazmatla, I whisper (it is a word I have made up), *Kazmatla. I believe. Life is red, it is many colors.* Beyond these words is a private dance. It is as silent as that.

I went one midnight to the geometric gardens. Lakelight, the moon on lake, brought out the depths of their colors and I stood close to where some dark water trickled through concrete slots. I could see only the red midnight flowers and the black basins of the fountains behind them. The flowers smelled stronger from a distance than they did right under the nostrils. Cinnamon and honey, acid.

I bent down over the water slots and shouted something, and the syllables were liquid syllables; they flowed down and away, out of the garden, toward the lake. They became the lake. I felt myself proceeding with ease from one reality to another, imagined myself creating and destroying each world of sensation I encountered.

Some time later I boiled eggs and ate my thin volumes of verse like fragile lettuce sandwiches. Then I think I wrote again with raving sanity: "The lake claims my face, the work of the surf is my body; I must remember those orderly, censured gardens. . ."

I have begun to repair the house, having put it off for ages, deciding which aspect of it was most in need of repair.

Of erections, how few are domed like St. Peter's? I ask myself (Melville), as I hammer nails into the tottering walls.

Are there too many realities? I ask, as several of the nails fall out.

Art is affirmation; to lift the pen is to say Yes! I cry, as the wall and I support each other.

Then I begin to bring the outside in, that the house might be a small, select museum of the world. In the summer I bring driftwood, shells, flowers. There is no key to this place and, in a sense, no door. There is free passage in and out. Already small weeds shoot up between the floor and the wall. . .

I tack up wallpaper that looks like wood (the walls were wood in the first place until the previous tenants covered them with dainty indoor scenes). I consider embroidering excerpts from the Cabbala on the cushion covers, or crocheting the writings of Kazantzakis on the tea-cosy, but I have no patience for such things. It seems I have one foot in one world and the other foot in another; I think I need new shoes.

Melville, it is said, read books about whales using whale-skins as bookmarks . . .

When the ice-sheets groan and split on the lake they fracture the landscape for miles around. Today I bless the authors of our borders and boundaries — Columbus who I sometimes imagine anchored in mid-sea with America moving out like a great ship to discover *him*. Vast shorelines, tongues of continents like land-waves chasing the seas. Shorelines of souls, the beaches of consciousness strewn with a thousand little shells. . .

The warehouses in the harbor turn gold at sunset; strange ships might sail in now from exotic foreign lands carrying ostrich feathers, elephant tusks, spices, silver filigreed bracelets, quinquiemec . . . The snow-capped coalpiles are a mountain range in Tibet. Sundog the cat enters the house with snow on his eyebrows. All is well with the world. Somewhere out on the breakwater a single gull is preparing for some ultimate flight. Everything begins, everything is a continuum, everything organizes its death. There are red midnights of flowers, there are white midnights of snow. There are no alternatives to pain, there are no alternatives to beauty. The lighthouse describes great cryptic arcs across the darkness. We fold in upon ourselves like the waves, we fold under, falling in and out of the world's vision. How many languages can we know? We approach the end of utterance.

Kazmatla, Kazmatla, the waves insist it has all been said before. Somehow they must convince me, somehow I must believe them. The body has its own speech to be heeded now. Move swiftly in these snows, and leave no track.

From THE T.E. LAWRENCE POEMS

The T.E. Lawrence Poems were published by Mosaic Press in 1982.

Writing in the first person MacEwen recreates Lawrence from childhood to death. She understood Lawrence's politics, but in the sequence is most interested in what she would call the mystic aspect of his personality and in the despair of disbelief. Of the poems, MacEwen said in a radio broadcast:

"The figure of Lawrence has always fascinated me. Lawrence was drawn to the desert Arabs, the Bedouin, among other things by the fact that they felt such great joy in renouncing the pleasures of the world. It was almost a voluptuousness in not having anything, not owning anything, and their relationship to their god was a passionate one. Lawrence was consciously in awe of this, could never achieve it himself, and I feel the same way. This is one of the reasons I wrote the book in the first person, myself as Lawrence. Looking upon this marvellous religious phenomenon and not being able, quite, to participate in it. Knowing however what it means. I feel much more of a mystically minded person than Lawrence was. I feel perhaps closer to this kind of passionate fervor the desert Semites felt towards their god in this vast nothingness. . . to Lawrence they were only words that fascinated him, concepts that fascinated him, but didn't touch him."

WATER

When you think of it, water is everything. Or rather,
Water ventures into everything and becomes everything.
      It has
All tastes and moods imaginable; water is history
And the end of the world is water also.

                   I have tasted water
From London to Miranshah. In France it tasted
Of Crusaders' breastplates, swords, and tunnels of rings
On ladies' fingers.

         In the springs of Lebanon water had
No color, and was therefore all colors,

                    outside of Damascus
It disguised itself as snow and let itself be chopped
And spooned onto the stunned red grapes of summer.

For years I have defended water, even though I am told
        there are other drinks.
Water will never lie to you, even when it insinuates itself
Into someone else's territory. Water has style.

Water has no conscience and no shame; water
        thrives on water, is self-quenching.
It often tastes of brine and ammonia, and always
Knows its way back home.

When you want to travel very far, do as the Bedouin do —
Drink to overflowing when you can,

               and then
Go sparingly between wells.

MY MOTHER

In Dublin they called her The Holy Viper; she helped God
          to erase all sins except her own.
Knowing her means I'll never make any woman a mother;
Let them find something else to devour besides
          their own children.
She didn't care for girls in the house, they weren't her.

I never let her see exactly who I was and what I loved,
          for she would understand, and then I
          would have to also. She was illegitimate
          like me; it ran in our blood.

I was a standing civil war for as long as I remember,
Trying to contain both her and my father, and now
          I am a castle that she lays siege to;
          she aspires to its tower.

The Arabs say that Mother Eve is a giant who stands
          three hundred feet tall;
          if I raise myself to my full height
Then I can see her, green and powerful, gazing at me still.

OUR CHILD WHICH ART IN HEAVEN

The child leads the parents on to bear him; he demands
        to be born. And I sense somehow that God
Is not yet born; I want to create Him.

If everything were finished, and we could say
            we'd given birth to stars, if we could say
Give over, it's done — all would be wild, and fair

But it is not yet over; it has not yet begun.

God is not yet born, and we await the long scream
        of His coming. We want the water to break
So we can say: *In the Beginning was the Word.*

Meanwhile, if one must die for something,
            there's nothing like a cross
            from which to contemplate the world.

THE LEGITIMATE PRINCE

I was a flea in the legitimate prince's bed, the bed
Of he-who-was-not-me, he who had the real birthright.
He wore noble clothes,
                              and saved every damsel in distress
Within a hundred miles. His eyes and his scabbard shone.

He-who-was-not-me showed no mercy and no fear for any-
thing.
Lies glanced off his sword — shot light.
                                        Terror swooned;
He answered to no one, and claimed the world as his own.

He never looks anyone in the eye for fear they would fall
Into the well of his gaze and drown there, thrashing around
              like the fools, the pipsqueaks they were,
And he wanted to spare them.
                          All colors admired him, God
              admired him, God how I longed to become him.

But I was born on the wrong side of the bed, which made me
Prince of Nothing, and I fell off the edge of it into Hell.

MY HALF-SISTERS

Like the legitimate prince, they were legitimate princesses,
        (my father was actually married to their mother) —
And I, their bastard half-brother, used to imagine them
Crocheting doilies and toiling over impossible needlepoint
        in shadowy alcoves where their purple dresses
        fluttered, and their powerful and secret minds
        made mock of me and my bastard brothers.

One half of them was one half of me; I never could fathom
        what that meant. They were forbidden to me
        by blood, yet I felt them lurking, waiting
        to devour me just beyond my door.
My ghostly half-sisters, beautiful and cruel, were fond
Of tea and blueberry scones at ten past five, talked
        incessantly of me, and slowly got older.

Now I think they might drop a stitch when someone comes —
        a visitor or a casual friend — and asks them
        if their half-brother is really the uncrowned
King of Arabia. I wonder what they say to him,
        those odd, uncanny, women,
        my twilight sisters, guarded by unicorns.

MY FATHER

He never looked at anyone, not even me, like once
On one of those official city mornings, he stepped
       right on my foot in the middle of the road
      and kept on walking into nowhere.

He had inherited enough money for him to sail yachts
And shoot pheasants, and ride hard and drink hard
       until she tamed him with her fairy tales
      about God, and how He loved the sinner,
Not the sin. I wonder what he thought of his five
       little bastards. It was impossible to tell.

Now I'm very much like that country gentleman, in that
I can talk to you for hours without for a moment revealing
       that I don't have a clue who you are;
I never look at a man's face and never recognize one;
       I have never been sure of the color of my eyes.

Sometimes he looked so lost that I wanted to show him
The way back home, but the house had become a place
       of thunder; it stared at us with square,
      unseeing eyes, and I never knew why
He went to her in that permanent, resounding dark.

I suppose he might have been a lion of a man, but
When you castrate a lion, all its mane falls out and
       it mews like a cat. Imagine, he was afraid
      of everything; I, of nothing — (my key
      opened all the houses on the street, I thought).

Once as a boy I asked someone if a statue I stared at
Was alive. They said no, but they were wrong. It was.

IT WAS ONLY A GAME

As children my brothers and friends and I used to play
A very simple game. The good guys, knights in armor,
would lay siege to the castle held by the
bad guys who were holding some of our
good guys.
We of course had to free the
good guys from them, the wicked ones.

Or —

We could be the bad ones and hold the
fortress against the onslaught of the
good ones who were coming to get more
of their good ones from us.

Maybe it wasn't such a simple game. In any case,
Those hostages of high cities, prisoners of citadels
were real, and the castles containing them
were real, because we deemed them so.
We the saviours were rewarded with gold rings and huge
Banquets with boars' heads stuffed with fruit, oranges
Studded with cloves, and wine all over the place.

The wild clumsy summers of our play succumbed to Fall,
And then to long sullen winters.
I dreamed of having
Millions of people expressing themselves through me,
Of being the saviour of a whole race, of rescuing
A whole people from tyranny. Those were the tender,
obscene dreams of my childhood.

Alone at night in the breathing garden, I needed horses,
And limitless space. Everything awaited me — the world
and the world beyond.

I didn't see the enemy outside, scaling the garden walls.
How easily are we overcome, how cleverly are we
destroyed.

IN BED

One should only live in the future or the past,
In Utopia or The Wood Beyond the World, I said,
   but I had this Mission; it devoured
   my waking moments, and forced the present
   upon me like a storm.

I had a brass-rubbing of a dead Crusader on my ceiling
And when sometimes, in satin midnights,
         my flesh crawled
With unspeakable desires, and the wind teased
The silly trees,
   and I knew myself to be
Just one step short of perfect — I'd lie and stare
At that ridiculous hero,
      his lurid body eaten by worms,
Night after night above me.

ANIMAL SPIRITS

Is it true, then, that one fears all that one loves?
These spirits are my awful companions; I can't tell
            anyone when they move in me.
They are so mighty they are unclean; it is the end
Of cleanliness; it is the great crime.

I can only kill them by becoming them. They are all
I have ever loved or wanted; their hooves and paws
            smell of honey and trodden flowers.

Those who do not know me sip their bitter coffee
            and mutter of war. They do not know
            I am wrestling with the spirits
            and have almost won. They do not know
I am looking out from the camels' eyes, out
            from the eyes of the horses.

It is vile to love them; I will not love them.
                                        Look —
My brain is sudden and silent as a wildcat.
                                        Lord,
Teach me to be lean, and wise. Nothing matters,
            nothing *matters*.

THE CHILD AND THE CATHEDRAL

It was in the white light of a dreadful afternoon
        that I saw the child. She wore a bright
White dress and was playing with a ball in front
Of the cathedral. I knew
           she was animal; in my hatred
Of animals I began to balance her
              against the cathedral.

If I had to sacrifice one of them, I asked myself —
        which would it be?
            I knew it was
The cathedral. I would destroy it to save her.

Another time I swerved at sixty miles an hour
To save some damned little bird that dashed itself out
        against my side-car. Why did it have to
Kill itself against *me,* for God's sake, why *me*?

Don't they know their existence wounds me, don't
They know I am the victim of such loveliness
        I want to die in it and cannot?
Don't they know the hatred and fear and pity go on and on
And turn into love, horrible love that bashes
        its brains out against the light?

THE WATER-BEARER

On a hill at Carcemish which is in Mesapotamia, which is
        Between-The-Rivers,
We dug up the bones and artifacts of ancient strangers,
You and your donkey lugging buckets of water
        back and forth over many thousands of years,
While I made notes about absolutely everything, and
        wrote long letters home.

You watered the mules and camels and nothing was ever
Too pretty or tiresome that you couldn't make mad and
        silly fun of it;
                    everything admired you.
The animals admired you because you had a splendid
        disregard for man that even they
        could not achieve. And a dark and secret love
That only they could achieve.

When it was too hot, we swam, and then the river
Released us and found its way back home.

They called you Darkness although your skin was fair;
I gave you a camera and taught you how to explore
        the darkness that lived behind light;
You said you would take pictures of the whole world.

Water-bearer, you gave everything and asked nothing
        in return. We dreamed that one day
        the ghosts of your ancestors would arise
        and tell us wonderful Hittite secrets;
But we had forgotten that your name meant also

the darkness of water before Creation;
we did not know that you would one day drown
In the dark water of your own lungs.

I loved you, I believe. It was before the horror.

THE ABSOLUTE ROOM

We came to a place which was the center of ourselves
   in the desert between Aleppo and Hama;
We came to this Roman place where a hundred scents
   were built somehow right into the walls.
So the old man and the boy led us through courts
   of jasmine, and many other flowers, then

Into this great hall where all the scents slayed
   each other, and were still, and all
We breathed was pure desert air.

       We call
  this room the sweetest of them all,
You said.
    And I thought: *Because there is nothing here.*

I knew then that you possessed nothing of me, and I
   possessed nothing of you, Dahoum.
We were wealthy and stuffed with a wondrous nothing
   that filled the room and everything around.

You looked into my eyes, the windows to my soul,
   and said that because they were blue
You could see right through them, holes in my skull,
   to the quiet, powerful sky beyond.

THE DESERT

Only God lives there in the seductive Nothing
That implodes into pure light. English makes Him
        an ugly monosyllable, but Allah breathes
A fiery music from His tongue, ignites the sands,
        invents a terrible love that is
The very name of pain.

The desert preserves Him
        as the prophets found Him, massive and alone.
They went there, into that awful Zero
                to interpret Him,
        for Himself to know, for He said: Help Me,
I am the One who is alone, not you. Tell Me who I am.

Camels lean into the desert, lost in some thought
        so profound it can only be guessed. When
Will God invent man? When
             will the great dream end?
My skin crawls with a horrible beauty in this
        Nothingness, this Everything —

I fall to my knees in the deep white sand, and my head
        implodes into pure light.

EXCAVATING IN EGYPT

Nobody knows how cold the nights can get in a land
Where sun is lord of the morning. It comes at you
        like a sword, the cold, and lays its side
        along your ribs;
                  there the flat steel sings
And you shiver under it, waiting for the dawn.

By day in Kafr Ammar we found trinkets of a people
Who lived there before the pharaohs — odd jewels
        and sad little things that could have been
        gods, or toys;
        Whatever they were, one played with them.

By night we grew fearful of these things; as the air
        grew more and more chill
        we gathered them up and returned to the tents,
        smelling of a thousand sweet, pungent spices,

Having wrapped ourselves in the funeral-cloths of the dead.

THUNDER-SONG

Two musicians played before the storm broke; one played
Wind-song, wind in the dry valley grass;
                                    one played
          dark, blind music on two strings. They both
Sang of war and love and death — what else is there
          to sing for?

Then came the armies of rain, wave after wave of it,
And a murderous blue lightning which brought the stones
          to life in the courtyard outside.
                                    Two lions
          on a pedestal laughed and laughed at us, with
          blue rain slobbering down their jaws, and then

Came the god, striding along an inscription towards the door.

The first musician controlled the thunder with his pipe
And the second explored the spaces in between
          the statements of the light.
                              In the place we were,
The place between twin rivers, Babylon, all was articulate
And utterly real.
                    Then the storm subsided and the pipe wept
At its passing. I knew that if ever I died it would be thus:

A helmetted seven-foot god coming quietly in blue light
Towards me.

APOLOGIES

I did not choose Arabia; it chose me. The shabby money
That the desert offered us bought lies, bought victory.
        What was I, that soiled Outsider, doing
Among them? I was not becoming one of them, no matter
What you think. They found it easier to learn my kind
        of Arabic, than to teach me theirs.
And they were all mad; they mounted their horses and camels
        from the right.

But my mind's twin kingdoms waged an everlasting war;
The reckless Bedouin and the civilized Englishman
        fought for control, so that I, whatever I was,
Fell into a dumb void that even a false god could not fill,
        could not inhabit.

The Arabs are children of the idea; dangle an idea
In front of them, and you can swing them wherever.
        I was also a child of the idea; I wanted
        no liberty for myself, but to bestow it
Upon them. I wanted to present them with a gift so fine
        it would outshine all other gifts in their eyes;
        it would be *worthy*. Then I at last could be
Empty.

You can't imagine how beautiful it is to be empty.
Out of this grand emptiness wonderful things must surely
        come into being.
When we set out, it was morning. We hardly knew
That when we moved we would not be an army, but a world.

ALI

Among the four sons of Sharif Hussein, in whose veins
Flowed the blood of the Prophet, I sought the man
who would lead his people against the Turks
      and on into Damascus.
Zeid was too young; Abdullah was jovial and too clever
For his own good.
      And then there was Ali, pious and clean
To a fault, Ali who loved beautiful things above all.

Often at dusk I'd catch him secretly smiling
      over the sheep heads that were also smiling
      on their beds of rice. He knew that I knew
He had thoughts too beautiful to be told. And once,
      he wrote to his Hashemite father, saying
How could his men advance on the enemy, without swords
      in scabbards of beaten gold?

Ali was not well; a delicate illness governed him
And made him a visitor, not a citizen of the world,
      and he talked much to his horses,
      and fondled them, which was something
I could never stand. It is not good to love and honor
      anything overmuch, as I have said.

Yet when I said goodbye to him once, we walked away
In separate directions, knowing that we understood
One another far more than either of us could say,
      and we were brothers just visiting the world.

FEISAL

He was standing in a doorway waiting for me, all white,
Framed in black, with the light
                              slanting down on him —
              a heavenly weapon.
Of the ten thousand and thirty-seven words for *sword*
              in Arabic, his name meant one:
The sword flashing downward in the stroke.

My lord Feisal, the man I had come to Arabia to seek,
Had a calm Byzantine face which, like an icon,
                    was designed to reveal nothing. Many times,
              I learned later, he had watched his men
              tortured by the Turks, and his black eyes
With their quiet fire did not flinch or turn away.

When he was at rest, his whole body was watching,
And when he moved, he floated over the earth, a prince.
                    Once when I saw him, dark against the sun,
                    its haze all gold through the silk of his *aba*,
I knew I would have sold my soul for him, joyfully.

And how do you like our place here in Wadi Safra?
                    he asked me, looking off to one side of me,
                    as though an angel stood there, listening.
Well, I said: *but it is far from Damascus.*

Later, when we rode northward into the dream that was his
And mine, he paid some of the men by letting them dip
                    their hands into a box of gold sovereigns,
                    and keep, not counting, all one hand could hold.

To reassure the others, he carried around false money —
Boxes of stones that rattled like silver and gold —
And we carried in our knapsacks the paper secrets
            that were war, the bundles of rotting letters,
            the green figs, the promises, the lies.

No matter what happened they would always adore him —
            the prince whose name was a sword —
And I would follow my lord Feisal from Wadi Safra
            to the ends of the earth.

AUDA

Auda was loud and lovely and his honor was more than gold
Among the Howeitat. No one could sing or ride like him;
       he ate the desert. He had slain seventy-five Arabs
        and Turks beyond counting, and the enemy was never
So lovely to him as when its life was his to take or give.
His heart was so huge it yearned towards the defeated one;
       I think at the moment he killed, he loved him.

As we sat in a circle at dinner around a pyramid of lamb
       and rice, he'd offer me the choicest chunks,
       and I'd give him some awful lump of guts
       in return, for Auda loved a damn good joke.
I made him laugh by telling his own stories better than he,
Of wild campaigns and how many men he killed — but always
Blood was blood; it was always red, only growing darker
       when it staled.

One night at dinner he got mad and stomped outside the tent
       and tore his false teeth from his mouth
       and did a little jig on them upon a rock
       because they offended him; a Turk had made them.
Later, when the night grew cold and we drank coffee,
I remember him musing: *Why do Westerners want everything?*
       Behind our few stars we can see God
       who is not behind your millions.
I said: *We want the world's end, Auda.*

He had twenty-eight wives, but only one son alive,
And one night I came across him in his tent, fucking
       one of his new wives, a jolly girl.

I was shocked that he took that awful comical
process of life so seriously. *Why, Auda?*
That's all I asked him — *why?*
And he said he wanted sons. Why did Auda want sons, why
Did anyone want sons, why did I have to walk in on Auda,
Magnificent Auda, and see him riding a woman like a fool?

Her lips were blue and her breasts were pointing to heaven;
She was enduring that unbearable humiliation to get a child.
  She ran away, what else could she do,
  and the wind whistled down the wadi
  and the exhausted camels roared.
Afterwards, I laughed at Auda and he laughed a little too,
  but he looked at me sideways and I knew
  that he knew something I didn't know
  and have never known.
It was colder than ever that night in Wadi Ruum.

NITROGLYCERINE TULIPS

We planted things called tulip bombs to knock out
        Turkish trains, or curl up the tracks;
        the Turks were so stupid, it sometimes
        seemed to me too easy. How could they
        expect a *proper* war
If they gave us no chance to honor them?

I called myself Emir Dynamite, and became quite deft
        at the whole business of organized
        destruction. In the back of one train
        which I derailed, was a carriage full of
        dying men; one whispered *Typhus,*
So I wedged the door closed and left them in.

Another time I straightened out the bodies of dead Turks,
        placing them in rows to look better;
        I was trying, I think, to make it
        a neat war. Once there were three hundred
        of them, with their clothes stripped off,
And I wanted nothing more than to lie down with them,

And die, of course — and think of nothing else but
        raspberries cold with rain, instead of
        sending currents into blasting gelatin
        and watching the sad old trains
        blow sky high
With Turks in little bits flying around everywhere.

SOLAR WIND

It comes upon you unawares —
                                something racing out of the edge
Of your vision, as when you are staring at something
            and not staring — looking through —
A herd of white horses grazing on the periphery
Of your sight, and the afternoon
                                slanting into night —

Comes the wind that is
                        the color of the sun, and your eyes
            which are nuggets of gold follow it
            down the barrels of the rifles, through
            the gun-cotton, and over the culverts,
Leaving everything gold, gold in its wake.

The past and the future are burning up; the present
            melts down the middle, a river of wind,
            wind from the sun, gold wind, anything —
And suddenly you know that all the mysteries have been solved
            for you, all questions answered.

You must find a god to worship or you will die
In that unholy moment just before darkness and the sound
Of guns.

DERAA

I started to write something like:
The citadels of my integrity were lost, or
            quo vadis from here, Lawrence?
                                    How pathetic.
I may as well tell you that as a boy my best castle
            was besieged and overcome by my brothers.

What happened of course was that I was raped at Deraa,
            beaten and whipped and reduced to shreds
            by Turks with lice in their hair, and VD,
            a gift from their officers, crawling all over
            their bodies.
                        I had thought that the Arabs were
Bad enough. Slicing the soles of a prisoner's feet
            so that when they let him return to his men,
            he went very, very slowly;
                                    but they were merciful.

Imagine, I could never bear to be touched by anybody;
I considered myself a sort of flamboyant monk, awfully
            intact, yet colorful.
                        Inviolable is the word.
But everything is shameful, you know; to have a body
            is a cruel joke. It is shameful to be under
            an obligation to anything, even an animal;
            life is shameful; I am shameful. There.

So what part of me lusted after death, as they smashed
            knees into my groin and turned a small knife
            between my ribs? Did I cry out or not when

they held my legs apart and one of them rode
upon me, laughing, and splitting open
a bloody pathway through my soul?
I don't remember.
                        They beat me until something, some
primal slime spilled out of me, and fire
shot to my brain.
                        On a razor edge of reality,
I knew I would come out of this, bleeding and broken,
        and singing.

THE REAL ENEMIES

In that land where the soul aged long before the body,
My nameless men, my glamorous bodyguards,
                                    died for me.
My deadly friends with their rouged lips and pretty eyes
          died for me; *my bed of tulips* I called them,
          who wore every color but the white
          that was mine alone to wear.

But they could not guard me against the real enemies —
Omnipotence, and the Infinite —

                         those beasts the soul invents
          and then bows down before.
The real enemies were not the men of Fakhri Pasha, nor
Were they even of this world.
                    One could never conquer them,
Never. Hope was another of them. Hope, most brutal of all.

For those who thought clearly, failure was the only goal.
Only failure could redeem you, there where the soul aged
          long before the body.
You failed at last, you fell into the delicious light
          and were free.

And there was much honor in this;
                         it was a worthy defeat.
Islam is surrender — the passionate surrender of the self,
          the puny self, to God.
We declared a Holy War upon Him and were victors as He won.

THE DEATH OF DAHOUM

Once I said it was as though you assumed the world
            while you lived, took it upon yourself
            lightly, like a cloak — but now
I think it was the world which borrowed you for a time
And then let go.

No one was there when the world began for you, Dahoum,
            and I was not there when it ended,
            when your lungs filled up with water
            and water filled the dark well of your mouth.
Once I could have drowned in your liquid eyes, forever.

I had this gift for you — the freedom of your race. But
            you come in dreams to tell me
            it was wasted; and in those dreams
            you wear your death well, gracefully.

What would you have said — and in what tongue —
            had you been able, when you died,
            to speak?

TAFAS

We came to the village after the Turks. Everyone was
                                                    dead,
Except a little girl who came out from the shadows
                                                    with
A fibrous hole gaping where her neck and body joined;
                                                    she
Cried *don't hit me, Baba,* then hobbled away and fell

Down in a little heap.
                    And then, I think, she died.

Death's little silver cock was struck
                                between her mother's legs;
She sat on the tip of a saw
                            bayonet. And a pregnant woman
Was bent over a sheepfold,
                        the hilt of Hell's sword
Sticking up from where
                    the fetus was, into the air.
                                        And others
Were pinned by legs and arms to the ground like
                                            insects
Mounted by an insane collector.
                            We went after the Turks
And killed them all.
                    Then we blew in the heads of the animals.
The sweet salt blood
                of the child ran out and out
                                    and on and on
All the way to Damascus.
                        All this happened as I have said, and
The next day was Friday.

A PHOTOGRAPH FROM CARCEMISH

I gaze at you now, my darling, my brother,
      the pistol asleep in your young groin,
      your lips pulled back in a mighty grin.
My little Hittite, after you there can be no other.

In your dark eyes, my darling, my brother,
The world was created from the waters of Chaos;
      now black waves of tears
      crash upon the beaches of my sleep
      and drown my dreams forever.

Dahoum, Dahoum, Dahoum!

DAMASCUS

The dream was dead in me before we reached Damascus;
    it died with your death, and dead love
Was all I carried around with me in the clumsy luggage
    of the desert. But I remember
Entering the city, and the air silk with locusts;
    there was the smell of eternal cookies baking,
And someone ran up to me with a bunch of yellow grapes.

In the crowds, the Arabs smelled of dried sweat,
    and the English had a hot aura of piss
And naphtha. For some reason I noticed a sword
    lying unused in a garden, a still garden
Behind a palm tree. And the worthless Turkish money
    was flying crazily through the air.
Later, in the evening, the satiny white sand cooled
    my feet; nowhere else was there such sand.

That night the Turks and Germans burned what was left
    of their ammunition dumps.
They're burning Damascus, I said. And then I fell asleep.

TALL TALES

It has been said that I sometimes lie, or bend the truth
            to suit me. Did I make that four hundred mile
            trip alone in Turkish territory or not?
            I wonder if it is anybody's business
            to know. Syria is still there,
            and the long lie that the war was.

Was there a poster of me offering money for my capture,
            and did I stand there staring at myself,
            daring anyone to know me? Consider
            truth and untruth, consider why they call them
            the *theatres* of war. All of us
            played our roles to the hilt.

Poets only play with words, you know; they too
            are masters of the Lie, the Grand Fiction.
            Poets and men like me who fight for something
            contained in words, but not words.

What if the whole show was a lie, and it bloody well was —
            would I still lie to you? Of course I would.

CLOUDS HILL

Over twenty miles of broken heath and a river valley
Full of rhododendrons, the Prince of Mecca comes home.
        At least I think I am at home, but
        even the house is travelling somewhere —
        through time, I think, and beyond.
What is exotic? Home is more exotic than anywhere.
Walking to Clouds Hill, I see the trees get crookeder
        and crookeder; their branches bridge
        the night and morning. Herds of clouds
Erase the sunset; I inhabit the hard core of everywhere.

The wind is easing south; soon, shy stars will come.
Everything has designed itself — the planets know me,
        wind knows me, night knows me;
        Clouds Hill leans against the sky.
I'm awaiting something so important it will never be,
And in dreams I go south and south and south again:
        Damascus, Deraa, Amman, Jerusalem,
        Beersheba, Ma'an, Akaba, Wejh, Um Lej,
        Yenbo, Rabegh, Jidda, Mecca.

Feisal is dead; Bob and Mother are still spreading God,
        and the news from China is nil.
Some of my diaries were written in pencil, upside-down,
        and day after day I decipher them
        on a heavy oak desk.
I live on dark chocolate, and write about the War.

THERE IS NO PLACE TO HIDE

Here is a famous world; I'm standing on a stage
With ten spotlights on me, talking about how I detest
        publicity. I stand there like an ass,
        apologizing for having a past, a soul,
        a name (which one?), and then
        back shyly into the limelight.

No. What I'm really doing is standing in an unlit room
Holding a court martial upon myself. Shaw tells me
        that to live under a cloud
        is to defame God. I can neither reveal myself
        nor hide. No matter what I do, I am naked.
I can clothe myself in silk or chain mail, and I
        am naked; everything shows through
        and yet no one can see me.

Can you imagine that posterity will call me wonderful
        on the basis of a few pencil sketches,
        a revolt in the desert,
        and my irresistably foul soul?
Outside my window, a small tit bird bashes itself
        against the glass. At first I thought
        it was admiring itself in the window.
        Now I know it's mad.

NOTES FROM THE DEAD LAND

I have died at last, Feisal. I have been lying
On this hospital bed for five days, and I know
            that I am dead. I was going back home
            on my big bike, and I wasn't doing more
            than sixty when this black van, death camel,
Slid back from the left side of my head, and ahead,
Two boys on little bikes were biking along, and
            something in my head, some brutal music
            played on and on. I was going too fast,
            I was always going too fast for the world,
So I swerved and fell on my stupid head, right
In the middle of the road. I addressed myself
            to the dark hearts of the tall trees
            and nothing answered.

The Arabs say that when you pray, two angels stand
On either side of you, recording good and bad deeds,
            and you should acknowledge them.
            Lying here, I decide that now
            the world can have me any way it pleases.
I will celebrate my perfect death here. *Maktub:*
It is written. I salute both of the angels.

- Behold part of the violent skies...

Gwendolyn

From **AFTERWORLDS**

Afterworlds was published in April 1987, seven months before Gwendolyn MacEwen died.

This book was also rigorously organized, its six sections divided into "Preworlds" and "Afterworlds," but the pattern is not linear but circular: the poems mirror each other, images repeat. The last section "Avatars" are love poems, but MacEwen warns: "The male figure in many of my mystical poems is a combination of lover, deity, muse, angel and demon. Except for a few, they are not poems about frustration in love, not at all. It is much more complex than that." Many of the poems in *Afterworlds* are elegiac. But MacEwen added: "I fear death as I fear the traffic in the streets, the danger. . . but the time we call death is part of life and there is only life."

THE GRAND DANCE

I promised I would never turn you into poetry, but
Allow this liar these wilful, wicked lines.

I am simply trying to track you down
In preworlds and afterworlds
And the present myriad inner worlds
Which whirl around in the carousel of space.

I hurl breathless poems against my lord Death,
Send these words, these words
Careening into the beautiful darkness.

And where do all the words go?
They say that somewhere out there in space
Every word uttered by every man
Since the beginning of man
Is still sounding. Afterthoughts,

Lethal gossip of the spheres.

Dance then, dance in the city streets,
Your body a fierce illusion of flesh, of energy,
The particles of light cast off from your hair
Illumine you for this moment only.

Your afterimage claims the air
And every moment is Apocalypse —

Avatar, deathless
Anarchy.

THE WHITE HORSE

This is the first horse to come into the world;
It heaved itself out of the sea to stand now
In a field of dizzy sunlight,
Its eyes huge with joy and wisdom,
Its head turned towards you, wondering
                    why you are wondering

And how it comes about that you are here, when
Shrapnel from wars whose causes are forgotten
Has invaded the soft legs and bellies of children
And phosphorous bombs have made burnt ivory
                    of the limbs of lovers
In Ireland and Lebanon and all the broken countries
Of the universe where this horse has never been.

You reach out your hand to touch it, and
This is the first time you have ever seen
                    your hand, as it is also
The first time you have smelled the blue fire
Within a stone, or tasted blue air, or
Heard what the sea says when it talks in its sleep.

But hasn't the brilliant end come, you wonder,
And isn't the world still burning?

Go and tell this: It is morning,
And this horse with a mane the color of seafoam
Is the first horse that the world has ever seen,
The white horse which stands now watching you
Across this field of endless sunlight.

LATE SONG

When it is all over — the crying and the dancing and the long
        exhausting music — I will remember only
How once you flirted with your death and lifted your dark eyes
        to warn me of the world's end
As wild leaves fell, and midnight crashed upon the city.

But it is never over; nothing ends until we want it to.
        Look, in shattered midnights,
On black ice under silver trees, we are still dancing, dancing.

Meet me in an hour at the limits of the city.

THE DEATH OF THE LOCH NESS MONSTER

Consider that the thing has died before we proved it ever lived
     and that it died of loneliness, dark lord of the loch,
fathomless Worm, great Orm, this last of our mysteries —
     haifend ane meikill fin on ilk syde
     with ane taill and ane terribill heid —
and that it had no tales to tell us, only that it lived there,
     lake-locked, lost in its own coils,
waiting to be found; in the black light of midnight
     surfacing, its whole elastic length unwound,
and the sound it made as it broke the water
     was the single plucked string of a harp —
this newt or salamander, graceful as a swan,
     this water-snake, this water-horse, this water-dancer.

Consider him tired of pondering the possible existence of man
     whom he thinks he has sighted sometimes on the shore
and rearing up from the purple churning water,
     weird little worm head swaying from side to side,
he denies the vision before his eyes;
     his long neck, swan of Hell, a silhouette against the moon,
his green heart beating its last,
     his noble, sordid soul in ruins.

Now the mist is a blanket of doom, and we pluck from the deep
     a prize of primordial slime —
the beast who was born from some terrible ancient kiss,
     lovechild of unspeakable histories,
this ugly slug, half blind no doubt, and very cold,
     his head which is horror to behold
no bigger than our own;

no bigger than our own;
      whom we loathe, for his kind ruled the earth before us,
who died of loneliness in a small lake in Scotland,
      and in his mind's dark land,
where he dreamed up his luminous myths, the last of which was
man.

STONES AND ANGELS

for Yannis Ritsos

I tried to find a stone for you to paint on, Yanni,
          and I found that
Stones are lost sheep in golden dust
Stones are the blind eyes of lost gods
Stones are stars that failed and fell here
Stones are the faces of watches without hands,

Stones are the masters of time.

And we would become the masters of time, Yanni,
          in the great loneliness which is God,
In the mad, dynamic silence poems and icons adore.

We would paint the universe the colors of our minds
          and flirt with death, but
Whether we dance or faint or kneel we fall
On stones.

Stones are old money with which we rent the world,
          forgetting that the landscape borrows us
For its own time and its own reason.

The way is open, it is paved with stones;
They are the fallen eyes of angels.

Antiparos, Greece, 1976

THE GARDEN OF THE THIEVES

For years I have wanted to write a poem called
            The Garden of the Thieves.
The title turns up in old notebooks with asterisks
Surrounding it and arrows pointing to it, and
Notes telling me to write it, write it, but

It never got written until now because I never knew
            where the garden was, or who
The thieves were, so the naked title lay there
Between sheets of paper that seethed with reason
And grand ideas, until one night I actually dreamed

Of the garden where I played as a child, and it was
            invaded by *thieves*
Who stole the Great Poem from me, the one we all know
Never gets written, and I saw the title as they
Whisked it away, and yes, it was beyond a doubt

The Garden of the Thieves, written by Anonymous
            who was my favorite poet
And who I thought was a Byzantine king. I have been
Pondering over this for quite some time, and thought
I'd better get it all down before the night falls.

THE WAH MAI CAFÉ

There's nothing new here; it's just how you pay for it.

Actually *it's* not here anymore, but it was
Near a theatre where Blackstone made everything disappear
And an aging stripper made her tits circle simultaneously
In two opposite directions
And an androgynous angel they called Billy
Appeared at midnight.

So I'd go in my brown corduroy jumper and sit
And take notes because I Was Going To Be A Writer
And when one of the hookers Lily asked me what the hell
I was doing, I said I had to see the seamier side of life,
Etc. She said: You're OK, you can stay.

At the Wah Mai Café Lily would bum cigarettes off me
After she'd turned a trick down the lane
Until the night the cops raided the place and Lily said
Goodbye, Goodbye, as they took some pimps and hookers
away.

Who the hell are you, one cop asked me, gazing in disbelief
At my brown corduroy jumper. I Am a Writer, I said,
And I work at Boys and Girls House which is
A children's library. Actually I'm just a page
But one day I'm going to be a Book.

For Christ's sake go home, said the cop, so I left
And I'm telling you, would I lie to you, it was wonderful
And awful, me and Lily and the others in the Wah Mai Café

All going out into the seamy night in opposite directions,
Some of them disappearing down the lane, me hopping a streetcar,

All of us trying to find our way back home.

BUT

Out there in the large dark and in the long light is the breathles
Poem,
As ruthless and beautiful and amoral as the world is,
As nature is.

In the end there's just me and the bloody Poem and the murder
Tongues of the trees,
Their glossy green syllables licking my mind (the green
Work of the wind).

Out there in the night between two trees is the Poem saying:
Do not hate me
Because I peeled the veil from your eyes and tore your world
To shreds, and brought

The darkness down upon your head. Here is a book of tongue
Take it. (Dark leaves invade the air.)
Beware! Now I know a language so beautiful and lethal
My mouth bleeds when I speak it.

LETTERS TO JOSEF IN JERUSALEM

i

Josef, twenty years have passed since we sat in the cemetery close to No Man's Land, on somebody's gravestone, in a garden of death in Jerusalem, and the ancient night contained our youth. Though we were younger and older than death, and wise as the night was. All wars, we said, are born here in the City of Peace, and Jerusalem is not a city but a whore; thousands have taken her but she has only changed hands.

Do you remember

How the moonlight slayed us, its light a knife between our ribs, and our knees and elbows gathered silver as we bowed down. Yet we would not kneel in that most unholy of cities; we sat on the eloquent stone watching the cats pass, apolitical, into No Man's Land. Only they ignored the borders, only for them had the city never been divided. The washing which had hung for centuries on the clotheslines was still not dry, and

The Hebrew God was a string of names in the night.

Beneath the killing moonlight in the garden of tombstones, you said that in the East you are always walking on somebody's grave, and crackling static from a dying radio filled the night with rumors of wars fought and yet to be fought — all that old news, that up-to-the-minute history. Sandbags and barbed wire divorced the Old and New Jerusalem, and history was a veil the color of old blood over the valley between. There was music from a wedding;

Fools have always danced too close to the border.

I'm sending these letters to your old address in the New Jerusalem; now there is one Jerusalem, but we know that is an illusion; the whore belongs to no one for any length of time. What is sure is the passage of cats through their easy kingdom. Do you still live there? Are you alive or dead in the awful holy city, killed in the war that declares itself forever? Twenty years have passed and we're still sitting there, Josef, younger and older than death, discussing the endless names of God, Lord of a nameless world, looking out over the valley black with blood, over the vivid darkness of No Man's Land

To the divided city.

ii

What time is it now on the beach at Jaffa?

Remember that Arab boy who knocked my breath out early one morning? He asked me the time and I told him, then he threw me to the ground and crashed to his knees and held me down until my wrists throbbed. I noticed his fine white teeth, and the old houses, deserted and two-dimensional like studio props against the turquoise backdrop of the sea. The sun did not shine on those walls — it roared. And the Mediterranean had a deep pulse

Like the beat of a giant clock.

The beach was crowded with fish-skulls, and how violent the sun was! We kicked and thrashed and cursed, each in his own separate tongue. All I did was give him the time and all Hell broke loose; kids emerged from behind the walls trailing kites, and surrounded us, cheering. My braids, my shorts, my naked Anglo-Saxon knees had offended him, I learned later. Another time, in a village outside of Jerusalem, I was mistaken for a sabra and stoned by small Arab boys, so I walked around for weeks with a hole in my head.

How easily one becomes the enemy.

Josef, have you noticed that a thin film has settled over everything? You peel it away and the world is a raw nerve, throbbing and throbbing, even the stones are throbbing. There is nothing but this throbbing, this ancient pulse. If you see that boy on the beach at Jaffa, tell him the time. It is two minutes to midnight, though it feels like morning. The first battle of this war has begun on the beach at Jaffa. All battles begin on the beach at Jaffa. The sea is booming out the real hour of the world:

It is countdown; it is the same time everywhere.

iii

Do you still write your angry avant-garde plays?

I have the photo you sent me, of actors with mime-white faces all dying in different ways. Some go all limp and funny, they give up their hold on reality; others just die like clocks, they wind down. You always loved irony; there was that play about the man in the British army fighting the Nazis, then in the Irgun fighting the British.

It was the folly, you wrote me, the *foolness* of it all.

We sat all night long and listened to your friends play jazz on the roof of the theatre where you lived; we discussed how modern drama differed in the East and West. You said an old writer had called you a beatnik and tried to rough you up. Kids down in the streets below us screamed in the lost dialects of Babylon. I had just seen Kirk Douglas in *Spartacus* speaking Hebrew. You said — Look at the children, why

Do we keep making the beautiful children?

There was a beggar you tried to befriend, but he screamed "God will burn you!" when you offered him money or cigarettes. He had seen his family consumed in a village in Iraq and they had never stopped burning. In the West, you said, you hunger for violence; you flirt with it. In the East we have it;

That is the difference.

And years later you write to tell me politics does not matter, only theatre. Night falls like a dead bird or a dusty curtain. Are the kids still screaming in the streets below you? Tell them to stop, tell them all to stop and watch your mime-white clowns dancing down the foolish night, playing live, playing dead, playing everything that is allowed in the theatres of war.

The folly, Josef, the foolness of it all.

iv

This is a story, a letter and a dream.

You go into the desert, looking for the ten lost tribes of your mind. The bus is crammed with laughing sabras, their rifles slung over their shoulders. A Bedouin with a transistor radio under his black robes listens to ambiguous news from Jerusalem. The bus goes into the Negev. In Beersheba your wicked black camera aims itself at an Arab woman and her child. She demands money for whatever part of their souls you intend to steal. She suckles her child, her magnificent dark breast exposed: it is as though the child is suckling the night. She turns away from the camera;

It is her face she wishes to hide.

(You write to tell me you have joined the army because you must. The men are circulating a funny joke about Arabs and hyenas; some Arabs think that hyenas are succubi who jump on a man's back and suck his brains out so he goes crazy. In madness he will never enter heaven. The army considers loosing a pack of hyenas on the Arabs if other weapons fail. Laughter abounds. The Arabs have turned back in terror, leaving the desert full of shoes. You and your men, you add, have pushed on to Sinai, and

You have just dipped your foot in the Suez Canal.)

Here in the desert you go mad; death triggers the madness. The sand turns to water, to golden snow. The lost tribes dance in a horrible mirage in front of your eyes. Then evening falls and black sand veils your skin; the arid night will suck you in. Death stutters its idiot message in the throats of the guns. Death has sucked your brains out: no one will enter heaven now. The hyenas are all laughing at some sick joke as you leave the desert behind. The bus is crammed with cameras and radios.

It is just a few minutes to the end of the world.

v

And when it ends, when we finally break the Law —

The stars retreat, the trees fall into fire, the bones of antelopes are found among the rivers, the waters flow back-wards, the spines of the sea are broken. The universe dis-owns us; through forests of missiles

We come to the Dead, the speechless Sea.

Desert saints died on their knees here; they loved, and their love was a holy wound carved by God who lusted for their bodies and their minds, who claimed and kidnapped them — the thin Essenes, the wise men holier than air. The fire in their souls ignited us and we tried to love, but

Our love was a black love born of sorrow,

An unholy wound we carved in God, a gash in the cosmos where the final void oozed in. Unable to love the smallest things we let fall singing through our hands — lucid ani-mals and birds and flowers — to cherish life after birth, we gave birth to this death.

We announced the coming of a terrible kingdom and it came.

The parched sea drains, the caves give up their dehydrated
scrolls, cylindrical coffins of words, parchment auguries.
The prophecies are gasps, the dry white sounds of death.
Enraged by wounds we cannot heal, and blind with fear
which has become as true and usual as breath, we give our-
selves over to the lords of death. The Law is broken; we
enter

The kingdom. We come to the Dead, the speechless Sea.

vi

Josef, all my letters to you are lies.

In Jerusalem and Tel Aviv and Beirut there are children at
recess wearing many colors, there are beggars with the
world scooped out of their eyes, there are khaki-colored
walls, Yemenites selling thread, matches, combs, soap, nee-
dles, ribbons; everyone is hammering or cooking or selling
beer and halvah and kebab and felafel. There are pink and
gold walls and everything is full of the sweet conflicting
smells of leather, and bread baking

Thousands of years.

Over Beirut jets send out bright globes of heat to disperse
the missiles, as they dive into the pink and gold morning.
This day escalates into Nuclear Night. Things do not fall
apart; it is worse: everything is fused in an awful centre. The
people of Hiroshima did not have time to die; they melted.
In Jerusalem and Tel Aviv and Beirut the street vendors have
nothing left to sell, and all the colors of the many-colored
children

Burn into one.

The dead of the earth are masters of the night; they slide
sideways into our dreams. They are the bloated white
corpses of Sabra, fat as larvae, the four hundred bodies float-
ing years ago down the Mekong River, roped together like
ancestral memories, they are the saints and guerrillas on
wooden crosses, they are the dead of history and the dead of
this moment. I want to say all the dead of the earth sleep in
peace somewhere, their eyelids covered with Roman coins.
But that is not true; that is poetry. The truth is Nuclear
Night, the truth is

Shatila, fat with death, the broken horses.

vii

But there are moments when we dare to believe Peace —

Moments held in the spaces between other moments, like
the blue and red glow in the sections of Chagall's windows
in Jerusalem, moments when the world is in holy commu-
nion with itself. A moment hanging breathlessly over the
waters of Galilee, the sea which is not a sea, the groves along
the shore dark with summer,

The cool, miraculous waves of Kinneret.

A moment in a small hotel with an old man who was a
sheriff in the Wild East, talking of Lawrence and Palestine,
and the radio tells us a new satellite has been launched at
Cape Canaveral. He is almost deaf, so I point to the dark
skies above Galilee and make circles with my hand. All the
wars he has fought

Retreat into the silence of space.

A moment reading Engel's *Dialectics of Nature* in a small room in Jerusalem. "The dialectical immutability of matter . . . it can neither be created nor destroyed." In my mind, the Koran echoing: "The eternal God; He begetteth not; neither is He begotten."

A moment in late afternoon in mystic Safed,

When the passionate light shines on purple grapes, yellow beer, the green and violet slopes of Mount Miron. Giant insects with golden shells walk through my room and the pale-faced Hassidim, God dancing in their heads, talk quietly in the streets. And through it all, Chagall's mules and donkeys with velvet eyes wander around everywhere. All these moments, and the sun blasting the windows in Jerusalem,

Breaking the glass into perfect nuclei of light.

viii

History is wearing thin, Josef; soon there may be no more history.

This comes back to me: I told you how I joined a religious group on Mount Zion and we went into the Room of the Last Supper and fell on our knees and I prayed and then rose to an epidemic of cameras. Everybody photographing each other saying cheese in front of the ancient pillars and walls. I wondered how the pictures turned out; I never saw them. The priest kept reminding us that This Place Is Holy, and signs said:

The Enemy Is Watching You.

Eyes stared at us through binoculars; Israeli soldiers threw cigarettes to the Arab sentries; they were close enough to spit from one side of the border to the other. But you go any closer and you get your head blown off, we were told, because The Enemy Is Watching You. Which enemy, I asked you, Josef — the sentries, the Antichrist, Moloch, or

Our true selves, trapped in the undeveloped film?

I have your last letter in front of me now. You write: "Something very funny happened. Now this moment when I'm sitting and writing you, remembering our walk near the walls of the Old City, suddenly the Arabs begin to shoot. From my window I see that it's going to be a big fight — bombs, guns and all the rest of it. You see it's very interesting here in our Bloody Holy Land.

With the name of Jerusalem, Youssy."

That place where you live is not a city but a meaning; it is the conscience of the world. You cannot destroy her or forget her, you told me, she will make you return. Now I look back and see her stretched out like a gold spider over the hills of Judah; the walls of the Old City melt and sizzle in the distance. Perhaps it is not there at all.

From my window I see that it's going to be a big fight.

Will you write me back? *We are still young, and everything is a moment away from being destroyed*. Do you still live up there on the roof of the old theatre? *Lord, lead us out of this impossible night*. Do you still take walks through the graveyard where we sat? Twenty years have passed and we're still sitting there, Josef, younger and older than death, looking out over the vivid darkness of No Man's Land

To the divided city.

MANITOU POEM

"To enter this world was to step into, not out of, the real world."
— Selwyn Dewdney, *The Sacred Scrolls of the Southern Ojibway*

So I must stand away from the stone to enter the stone,
To dream the idea of the stone, the stone which is all stones,
          the first and final stone,
Its source being, its manitou.

As in puberty I dreamed my lifelong protector, who showed me
How to navigate impossible rivers, who made me as the world's
          first person, breathing
Fire and poetry.

The strangers who divided the world into good and evil were wrong
The Great Lynx Misshipeshu who dwells beneath ambivalent water
          is both benevolent
Lord, and devil.

And I am become the powerful dreamer who dreams his way throug
To reality, to enter and ignite the stone, to illumine
          from within
Its perfect paradox, its name.

GREY OWL'S POEM

There is no chart of his movement through the borrowed forest,
A place so alien that all he could do with it
        was pretend it was his own
And turn himself into an Indian, savage and lean,
A hunter of the forest's excellent green secret.

For all his movements through the forest were
In search of himself, in search of Archie Belaney,
        a lone predator in London
Telling the very king: *I come in peace, brother.*
(The princess thinking how alien he was, how fine.)

Stranger and stranger to return to the forest
With the beavers all laughing at him, baring
        their crazy orange teeth
And the savage secret — if there ever was one —
Never revealed to him. Stranger and stranger to return to

The female forest, the fickle wind erasing his tracks,
The receding treeline, and the snowbanks moving and moving.

THE NAMES

We want to pretend that you are our ancestors —
        you who are called
Wolf in the Water, Blue Flash of Lightning, Heaven Fire,
        Black Sleep —

You who have no devil, no opposite of Manitou.

You who are hiding behind your names, behind
        closed doors of thunder
And will not let us in.

Backlit by blue lightning, the silhouette of the wolf
        drinks the midnight river; fire from heaven
Falls on our sleep and invents morning; the air is thick
        with feathers from surreal birds.

You who never knew the evil in us, you who have
        no opposite of Manitou,
Come out from behind the thunder and embrace us —
All we long to become, all we have never known of ourselves.

Before you are gone from our eyes forever —
        (you who are certainly not our ancestors)
Teach us our names, the names of our cities.

No one ever welcomed us when we came to this land.

THE NAME OF THE NIGHT

The name of the night our mouths nibbling
the dark bread of love the dark flowers of love

The name of the night birds flying in all directions
dropping crumbs and petals on the world

The name of the night our mouths drinking
the dark wine of death the dark blood of death

The name of the night our bodies falling
a rain of wine and blood at midnight falling

The name of the night the black mouth of Africa
the open cavernous mouth of Africa

The gaping bird mouths of the dead of Africa
mute roar of the dark children across the land

SEEING EYE DOGS

For Barbara

If my cat sits long enough on my typewriter
She might write something wonderful.

Meanwhile the dog stars, the sundogs, those fake suns
Blind us who are addicted to light and dark, whose eyes
Are windows often peering into nowhere,
Into the phony houses of our lives,

While you and your black all-seeing dog
Lying in the corner of your room deflect me
From the gates of hell, then he
Leads you through the streets of this shady city.

Already I perceive the holes in my vision, the blind spots
I dare not face, I and my fellow fools
Glancing through day and night, dancing, adoring
The glare of our darkness.

Last night on TV Sherlock Holmes got into a carriage
Led by a horse with blinkers, and Sherlock's eyes
Went prancing, reflecting clues and theories
And focusing, finally, on the fact (surmise)
That the world was just as mad as he was.

And went home and shot up on something from the boredom
The boredom of it all.

Then I watched this fish with the craziest camouflage ever —
A phony eye at his tail so his enemies couldn't tell

If he was coming or going or what the hell
He thought he was doing.

So when I turn away from you I have eyes at the back of my head
Which allow me to see a world I've left behind —
And the dear creature who is your eyes
Lies regarding me with horror and surprise,
That I might glimpse reality perhaps once in a lifetime,

Or if my cat sits long enough on my typewriter
She might write something wonderful, sublime.

FIREWORKS

In memory of Marian Engel

A year after your death, in the spleen of winter
Part of your garden lies buried in my garden
Where I transplanted it. I wonder
Where you are now — (it isn't exactly heaven
because you said once you knew all about heaven
and didn't want to go there). Nevertheless
As I celebrate your life I celebrate your entry
Into some unconditional kingdom.

Friend, let your death be fireworks
Like the pinwheels and burning schoolhouses
(we have so much to unlearn)
You had in your garden on the 24th of May
A hundred years ago when we were less than young.

Let it be a conflagration, a sign,
Like all those loud outspoken flowers
Which will burn all summer in my back yard —
(the Japanese lanterns, bright audacious orange
against the garden wall) —

Everything struggling to become what it already is
And we who are left behind you
Struggling to become what we already are.

Winter 1986

EVA BRAUN REFLECTING, 1987

The blood has dried, the smoke has vanished, and the smell
of death is no more. They ask me what he was like in bed,
and I tell them I'd known better, I'd known worse; he was
adequate, considerate, a perfectly ordinary, normal lover.

Why
are they always surprised when I tell them that?

His mind wasn't black; it was white, white inside, a room
with white walls. If you went in you could learn nothing;
you knew as little as when you were on the outside; it was a
pointless exercise.

What
is so strange about that?

Marlene Dietrich told some guy who wanted her: I'll sleep
with you when Hitler's dead. Then after the war the guy
confronted her with her promise and Marlene said: Hitler's
alive and well and living in Argentina. Goodbye.

That
was so funny I laughed all night.

I heard that the British had a fighter pilot called Morning
Bird. He used to take off at dawn during the Battle of
Britain, and he had no legs. I sometimes think of him in the
cockpit — no legs, just wings.

Why
do I think about that?

I once knew a man who went to prison (this was before the war) for killing a young boy who wouldn't return his love. I went to visit him once in his dirty little cell and I was nervous in his presence. He said: Don't worry, I only kill on Thursdays.

What's
so important about that?

IN THE GARDEN OF THE CHELSEA ARTS CLUB

Alastair the poet tells me *nothing dies,*
        and in his eyes the great trouble of love
As he leads me through the garden gate
        where sunflowers grow tall as towers,
Past a little statue and a pool much gazed upon
        by Augustus John and others, sits down
And takes a nap and leaves me alone
        in the outrageous garden.

But endless time is the enemy, I thought,
        and suddenly at the far end of the garden
I locate the enemy in the form of the resident tortoise
        who is moving toward me sickeningly slowly.
Under the shell of the tortoise is the dark spirit
        of the garden, a naked thing
Devoid of anything, even hunger; it has not eaten
        for a hundred years
And still it is alive; it eats my eyes.

And Alastair who is 92 told me *nothing dies.*

The tortoise stares at a white petal with ferocious hatred;
        he cares for nothing but himself,
The world offends him, he is hideously sane,
        he has been in the garden
Since the beginning of time, and will be here forever,
        staring at nothing, staring at everything,
Blind.

But another white petal falls on his back from the tree
        and its weight is enough to kill him.
So beauty is your enemy, I discover, *you* will *die!*
        I leave the ridiculous, gorgeous, unreal garden
With the pool and the tortoise and the ghosts
        of Augustus John and others
And Alastair the poet, his eyelids slowly opening,
        eyes following me, eyes which will never really
Close.

London, 1984

LANGUAGES (2)

When we were fifteen my girlfriend and I used to sit in the back seats of Dundas Street streetcars and whip out our violins and play Bach's *Concerto for Violins in D Minor* all the way to Yonge Street. This was to startle people and make them notice us. Then we walked barefoot all over downtown before it became a fad in the Sixties, also to startle people and make them notice us. Some of these things worked, but the one thing that never worked was when we sat in the back seats of streetcars and spoke loudly in a language we made up on the spur of the moment, syllable by syllable. We didn't realize that in this country one more language, especially one more unofficial language would do you no good at all, although knowing only one language of any kind in this country would also do you no good; you had to know more than one to survive. All those mangled feet, all those wounded alphabets, all those illicit violins.

SUNDAY MORNING SERMON

The cat sits on the fence, turning into a bird, turning into a river, turning into an antelope. In the beginning the world was the sweet heart of nowhere; then everything became very articulate, which was marvellous considering nothing had a name. The lush exotic Nothing was crammed with forms and the forms were Something. Flowers brushed your legs, pleading with you to love them. They were red — no, red was the sound they made; actually they were blue and yellow. Now you can see as much as you choose; you can watch that tree as it sits there doing nothing, or watch that tree as it zooms through space. But if you think you are starting to know anything at all — beware. The cat has more surprises.

PAST AND FUTURE GHOSTS

Everything is already known, but we proceed as though we know nothing. I have lived in houses haunted by ghosts from the future as well as the past — ghosts of my future and past selves as well as ghosts of others. It's very simple; we all just move from room to room in these time-houses and catch glimpses of one another in passing. As a child in one house I used to see this older woman who was myself grown up, and thirty years later I went back there and met the child, who was waiting for me to come. Who is haunting whom? Right now some future ghosts are re-decorating the house I live in; I see them out of the corner of my eye, tearing down certain walls and inventing new ones. Look out — you who inhabit those rooms of my future — I'm coming after you. I'm starting to haunt you, I'm starting right now.

BARKER FAIRLEY AND THE BLIZZARD

It was freezing and wet and everybody was being blown all over the street and taking shelter wherever they could, when Barker emerged from the swirling cloud of the blizzard, walking slowly and thoughtfully, his cap at a superb angle. It was a few years ago, so he couldn't have been much more than ninety. *Gwendolyn,* he said, as the gale pushed me sideways and I crashed into a wall, *I've been thinking about suffering. Does the artist have to suffer, do you think? Yes,* I said. *Definitely. The older I get the more I suffer so it must be necessary. And furthermore it is packed with meaning.* Barker looked at me quietly as several people held onto each other's waists with the man in front attached to a telephone pole, to avoid being blown away. *I don't think so, I really don't think so,* he said, as two women and a man were washed into the gutter. *We're here to bring joy; we weren't meant to suffer at all.* And he leaned into the exquisite storm and was gone.

THE TRANSPARENT WOMB

Here's why I never had a child. Because down the lane
behind the Morgentaler clinic the mother of a tribe of alley-
cats nudges towards me the one she knows will die after its
first and last drink of warm water in the depths of winter,
because the bag lady down the street (who was once a child)
tells me she won't go on welfare because that's only for peo-
ple who are really hard up, because I collect kids and cats
and strangers (or they collect me), and at Halloween the poor
kids come shelling out and one boy wears a garbage bag
over his head with holes cut out for eyes and says does it
matter what he's supposed to *be*, and his sister wears the
same oversize dress she wears every day because it's already
a funny, horrible costume, hem flopping around her ankles,
the eternal hand-me-down haute mode of the poor, because

They wander into my house all the time asking "got any
fruit?" because their parents spend their welfare cheques on
beer and pork and beans and Kraft Dinner and more beer,
they won't eat vegetables with funny names like the Greeks
and the Wops, so the kids are fat, poor fat, fat with starch
and sugar, toy food, because

The kids in Belfast in that news photo were trying to pull a
gun away from a British soldier in a terrible tug of war
where nobody won, and

My foster kid in El Salvador is called Jesus.

Here's why I never had a child: Because they're so valuable I
could never afford one, because I never thought it was a

good way to glue a man to me, because I never thought I had to prove *I* could do it while they're starving everywhere and floating in gutters and screaming with hunger. All this in our time. All the world's children are ours, all of them are already mine.

THE MAN WITH THREE VIOLINS

Or you think there are three violins because there are three black cases strapped over his shoulder. You see him all the time on Bloor Street; he's carrying them somewhere, he's always been carrying them somewhere, years now. (Cats and dogs love him because animals love poets and musicians and anyone who breaks the law.) The truth is that if you opened the three cases you'd find in the first case: pages of thumb-prints of famous chess players, a collection of ancient Persian knives, authentic relics of the true cross, and little bottles of water from the Nile and the Thames and the St. Lawrence, and in the second case: Peruvian salt and pepper sets, cedarwood camels carved in Yemen, international stamps, so many you could mail anything from anywhere to anywhere, pebbles from Troy and the Parthenon, a napkin signed by Gregory Peck, and a scroll from Tibet. The third case is empty. Like his eyes. Full of lonely. An archive of nothing. There are no violins.

THE TIMING

Some days I cannot look at you,
I am dizzy with wisdom, I am struck dumb. Stars
Are fossils in space, the clocks of the city
Wind down. I tell all my poems to go home.

You slide through the slits of these minutes,
The thin air sliced by your presence, your perfect
Timing.

Help. I am numb with your beauty, I am
Besieged by truth.
Your hands are as lean as the long hours
Before midnight. Time
Is speechless as it strikes your mouth.

These preposterous lines proceed no further.

ABSENCES

You have never looked so fine
as now, when you are not here.

— So shot with light,
so sharply defined —

I cut my finger on the white
edges
of this paper.
I cut my eyes on the keen edges of your
absences.

I am faithless to you, distant one.
I lie with your blinding shadow, your

White mind.

A STILLNESS OF WAITING

"the stillness which I particularly associate with the Egyptians, a stillness of waiting, not of death."

— Henry Moore

How I long to return to you,
to enter the bright world of our youth.

I wear rings on the upper joints of my fingers
like those ladies from Pompeii. I wear
the red and blue and gold of Ur,
I wear the brutal jewels of Babylon.

The years crawl by like scorpions.

In the dusk and in the long shadows of the past I was
beneath your ribs, I was
between your legs, I was
inside your mind.

How I long to feel the dark voyage
of your hand along my spine.

How I long to return to you,
to enter the dark world of your mouth.

How I long for you my brother, my soul.

DAYNIGHTS

I don't trust you for a single second, but
My bones turn gold in your hands' warm holding
In the dark or in the bright heart of the morning,

And suddenly the days are longer than anything,
Longer than Tolstoy, longer than Proust, longer
Than anything.

But the days are also diving into night, and

I told you our end lay in our beginning
So we drink to our end, always remembering
That at the bottom of the goblets of Pompeii
Was the skull; we crawl

Out of the night utterly broken, bruises
All over our souls,

But this pain returns me to the world.

Even in the end your perfidy serves me, so
The cry we made when we came, love,
Will sound the same and is the same
As the cry we will make when we go.

LETTER TO AN OLD LOVER

Salah, I have not forgotten you.

It was you who claimed my only real virginity, you
who deflowered my mind, who ravaged my soul, whose
backwards tongue I learned and have since forgotten
except in dreams and on the wrong side of midnight,

Except when Arabic songs on the radio wail *habibi, habibi,*
our love is doomed, your father will not let us marry,
I daily die a thousand deaths, my tears pour out, and so on,

Except when I play tapes of Om Kalsoum who sang deep into
the Moslem night from Cairo once or was it twice a month
on Thursdays, and the whole Arab world high on hashish
wept and wailed and died as she sang *anta omri, you are my life.*

For five years we lay after love on a narrow bed and heard
the roar of Lake Ontario; you murmured of magenta flowers
and many stairs leading to the roof of your house in Giza
and the pyramids numb with night and time beyond the courtyard

I remember the taste of Egypt in your mouth —
mint tea and mangoes.

And the nights pouring in, the winter nights
pouring in, the magenta nights
pouring in,
the lake, the smell of your
far flowers.

Salah, are you sitting now on the roof of your house in Giza
under virginal moonlight, a lean and handsome man
approaching fifty with a wife and many children numb with
sleep after playing tag all day in the blazing courtyard?

Habibi, you are still my life, I murmur in that backwards tongue
as I climb the many stairs of midnight to encounter you,
*habibi, do you hear the roar of this northern lake, this
far country,*

*Do you hear the wail of the water,
the roar of our love, the old nights
pouring in . . .?*

NOVEMBER

If you knew that I would lie here on this dark November morn
Considering nothing but your eyes, your eyes,
Would you laugh with disbelief, surprise,
Remembering how we spoke of calculus and stars
And ruined civilizations and world powers
And their stupid chess games and unwon wars?

And how the innocence of this land may lie
Not in what we think is weakness, but in strength —
(What would they have called us if they thought
They'd found China instead of India —
Mandarins, Mongols, Chinks?)

And how at the end of the evening, Celestial
Tea was served, and I looked into your eyes, your eyes
And considered abandoning politics and poetry
For the dark spirits and spices of your body,
As subtle and alien and intimate and known to me
As you are, who are able
As all multiple and perfect equations are
To bend and break my mind?

I loved you. So sue me. A dozen stars
Went nova. Just like that.

THE LION

for Robert Duncan

To love is to be remarkable, and flawless.
It is to wear the yellow crown of a flawless beast
Forever.

It is to inhabit the flawless and exceeding universe
Forever.

It is to summon the wonderful numbers
Which add up to the mighty stars.
It is learning to divide and multiply by these numbers.

I swear by all the famous, ancient lions I have known
That the mighty children yet to come
Will foster finer stars,

For they are the true lords, born of morning
Whose coming will call us down
Like a deck of cards.

To love is to be remarkable, and flawless.
It is to wear the yellow crowns
Of all the gods.

MARINO MARINI'S HORSES AND RIDERS

So we embrace our end in our beginning.

All we have to give each other is
Our breath, our darkness breathing
Life into the dying lungs of the night.

Enter my darkness, I give you
My darkness;
Together for one second we are light.

We proceed in beautiful devastating stages
Towards our end, as the horse and rider
Collapse together in the catastrophe of love.

I lie in the night of your breath.
There is only your breath, all else has gone.

The horse dissolves between the rider's thighs,
The world dissolves before the rider's eyes.

So now, in the animal darkness, come.

A COIN FOR THE FERRYMAN

In this rain that lasts forever
I embrace a loneliness like no other
And live with it till it becomes my friend
And cast this savage poem upon the waters.

My love, I could not save you from your life
Nor you from mine, but I promise you these lines
Are as real as our names, as the pain we know
Of our coming and going, our swimming, our drowning.

The afterworld is the preworld, is this world,
Is the dawning when you are drawn taut as a bowstring
Or detached as a drawbridge, or are indeed
As liquid and lyric as a spear cast into water.

So I cast this ancient coin upon the waters
(Whose currency is long since cancelled) —
An offering to Charos who knows all too well
Of our coming and going, our swimming, our drowning

And will lead us both across the final waters.

THE TAO OF PHYSICS

In the vast spaces of the subatomic world where
Matter has a   tendency   to exist
The lord of Life is breathing in and out,
Creating and destroying the universe
With each wave of his breath.

And my lord Siva dances in the city streets,
His body a fierce illusion of flesh, of energy,
The particles of light cast off from his hair
Invade the mighty night, the relative night, this dream.

Here where events have a   tendency   to occur
My chair and all its myriad inner worlds
Whirl around in the carousel of space; I hurl
Breathless poems against my lord Death, send these
Words, these words
Careening into the beautiful darkness.

Contents

Acknowledgments

From *Afterworlds*, 1987, by Gwendolyn MacEwen.
Used by the permission of the Canadian Publishers,
McClelland & Stewart, Toronto, Ontario.

From the *T. E. Lawrence Poems*, 1982, by Gwendolyn
MacEwen. Used by permission of Mosaic Press, Oakville,
Ontario.